UNLEASHED

RELEASE
THE UNTAMED
WITHIN

UNLEASHED

ERWIN RAPHAEL McMANUS

THOMAS NELSON
Since 1798

NASHVILLE   DALLAS   MEXICO CITY   RIO DE JANEIRO

Published in association with Yates & Yates, LLP, Attorneys and Counselors, Orange, California.

Published in Nashville, Tennessee, by Thomas Nelson. Thomas Nelson is a registered trademark of Thomas Nelson, Inc.

Thomas Nelson, Inc., titles may be purchased in bulk for educational, business, fund-raising, or sales promotional use. For information, please e-mail SpecialMarkets@ThomasNelson.com.

Unless otherwise noted, Scripture quotations are from the HOLY BIBLE: NEW INTERNATIONAL VERSION®. © 1973, 1978, 1984 by International Bible Society. Used by permission of Zondervan Publishing House. All rights reserved.

Scripture noted NKJV is from the New King James Version. © 1979, 1980, 1982 by Thomas Nelson, Inc. Used by permission. All rights reserved.

Interior artwork by Joby Harris

Cover photo by Hank Fortener. Pictured: Mariah McManus

ISBN 978-1-4002-0254-6 (TP)

The Library of Congress has cataloged the hardcover edition as follows:

McManus, Erwin Raphael.
    The barbarian way : unleash the untamed faith within / Erwin
Raphael McManus.
        p. cm.
    ISBN 978-0-7852-6432-3 (hardcover)
    1. Christian life. I. Title.
    BV4501.3.M374 2005
    248.4—dc22

                                                                            2004027611

Printed in the United States of America
11 12 13 14 15 RRD 5 4 3 2 1

To Mariah, my Sweet,

Who loves to live and lives to love.
From first breath you have brought to life
both celebration and adventure.
Compassionate and courageous.
Delicate and determined.
Tender and tenacious.
Lover of God and lover of people.
You are both laughter and tears.
In ancient times, you would be the warrior princess.
Always follow the steps of the One who is scarred.
May we always choose the barbarian way,

Dad

But then the worst thing happened
that could happen to any fighter,
you got civilized.

—MICK TO ROCKY,
Rocky III

CONTENTS

Introduction

THE BARBARIAN WAY
UNLEASHED

I woke up one morning and my little girl had suddenly turned eighteen. It was in spite of my best efforts. Mariah insisted on growing up. So there I was in a conversation with my daughter about her future—some gibberish about needing to pursue her dreams and all that trendy stuff that, if left unattended, will corrupt the minds of our children. We live in Los Angeles, and for most teens that would be a dream come true. Where else other than New York or Paris can you go as an artist to live on the proverbial cutting edge? She was on her way to fashion school when she decided she needed to pursue her passion as a singer-songwriter. It was virtually the next day when *Grey's Anatomy* picked up a song she wrote when she was fourteen and recorded at eighteen. *Grey's Anatomy* featured it for more than four minutes during the pinnacle scene of their season finale. Mariah had been performing for years, but now her dream and direction were confirmed.

Mariah has an artist's soul with a pioneer's spirit. She also has a deep and rich spirituality. She has always been a reminder to me that a child can connect deeply to Christ with a profound maturity that transcends parenting. In other words, I don't know how Kim (her mom) and I raised such a great human being. Still, she has always had a tension between faith and fear. As a child, she always had a rich faith while strangely being afraid of everything—and I mean everything. She was afraid of the classics—the dark, being alone, flying, strangers, dogs, crossing the street, Barbie, Chuckie Cheese, Chip and Dale—you get the picture.

So when she came to me about her future, she said she needed to leave us and go to Nashville to write and record her new CD. Honestly, my first thought was, *what does Nashville have that LA doesn't have and better?* I also might have mentioned that if she stayed in LA, I would finance her project. But if she left me—I mean LA—she would be on her own. Once we worked it all out, we were saying goodbye to our little girl.

She was going without a place to live, without a producer, without a manager, without a studio, without any certainty. This daring plunge into the unknown was true to Mariah's soul. It is who she is. Then the fear set in. All the questions and doubts began to find a voice inside her head. She came to me just a few days before it was time for her and her mom to road trip across the country. Absent was the youthful enthusiasm and reckless abandonment she had expressed up to this point. Whenever she says, "Dad, can we talk?" I know it's going to be serious—or she wants clothes. Her discourse came down to three simple words— "Dad, I'm afraid."

Suddenly it all came crashing down on her, the realization that in just a few days she would be on her own. It's in those moments where as a dad you have to ask yourself, *what would Yoda say?* This time it was obvious. When she told me she was afraid, my immediate response was simply, "Then you have to go. You must never allow fear to establish the boundaries of your journey." Tears covered her eyes with a thin glaze, and without saying a word she hugged me. It was a nonverbal way of letting me know she was on her way to Nashville, fears and all.

When I first wrote *The Barbarian Way*, I dedicated the

book to my daughter, Mariah. It never occurred to me that the book would be dominantly seen as exclusively written to men. There was a reason why I dedicated it to my girl. For me she personifies the barbarian way both in her passions and her journey.

Whenever you choose to live a life of faith, even when it takes you into a world of uncertainty, you have made the barbaric choice. The reason this metaphor so resonated with me is because I saw how faith had become too civilized and its application too sanitized. There is something beautiful about a life lived in the simple belief that all we are meant to do is the outflow of faith, hope, and love. Mariah has always had a deep love for God and a simple trust in Christ. Jesus for her is her deepest love and everything in her life comes from that source. Of course that doesn't mean that she doesn't struggle with issues like fear and doubt; it just means she doesn't allow them to define her.

Looking back, it was appropriate that Mariah and Kim left Los Angeles, leaving me behind. Her mom never taught her how to cook, but she did teach her how to risk. It was not that long ago when Kim and Mariah had left me once before, headed to Zambia on a humanitarian mission. When you travel with Kim, you're less likely to stay in a nice hotel or eat gourmet meals and more likely to find yourself sleeping on hard beds and eating food you couldn't identify if your life depended on it. There are two undeniable characteristics that Kim passed on to Mariah—her height (or lack of it) and the spirit of the barbarian way. Kim is the powerful integration of a love for adventure, an insane willingness to risk, and a heart committed to serving the world. Whether in China or Indonesia working as an educator, in Mexico or Haiti doing relief work, or in LA building a home in South Los Angeles with Habitat for Humanity, Kim has never shied away from hard work or a difficult challenge. If anything, she seems to come alive when given the opportunity to serve in places where most of us would only be looking for the exit. She really is Joan of Arc under fire.

It was a Saturday morning and we were on our way to Mosaic's annual Leadership Advance. Kim all of a sudden informed me that we, that is, Mosaic, were going to participate as a congregation in the Habitat for Humanity project in South Los Angeles. My response was quick and clear, "That is simply not going to happen." She continued as if I had responded with an unhesitating affirmation of her new mission for my life. (It was one of those days that confirmed Kim has a severe hearing problem.) I just hate it when she springs things on me or when she expects me to introduce a new project to our community that has not been thought through and approved through the appropriate channels. That's a long and complicated way of saying *I need a process that backs me up when I say no to her.* But she was determined and had already made up her mind that this was going to happen.

Let me tell you that when Kim is resolved, you might as well get out of the way (or you'll get badly hurt) or pretend it was your idea all along because it's going to happen. After I took the first half of our trip to lay out every reason why this couldn't happen, shouldn't happen, and wasn't going to happen, she moved to what is her most devastating argument whenever she is about to lose. She just stopped talking, looked forward, and emanated the feeling of disgust. I had won. I wasn't about to concede. I was proud of the silence. It's good to let her think about what she's done and how she should do it differently in the future. Did I mention it was really, really cold in the car? I think it was September.

So I found myself in front of the leaders of our seven different locations as they eagerly awaited the vision for the new year. It turns out I was learning the vision with them instead of giving it to them. I suddenly found myself calling on all of our leaders not only to participate in a building project with Habitat for Humanity but also to *take on* the entire project ourselves. In the middle of a recession, in the middle of our congregation's difficult economic season, we decided to raise a $150,000 and build one house for one family. We needed to remind ourselves that while we may not be able to solve all of the world's problems, we could make a difference for at least one family. That day we raised more than $60,000 from the few hundred people that had come to find a new vision. That day was the catalyst for the greatest month of giving in the history of Mosaic. Facing double digit unemployment nationwide and having seen our budget decrease 25 percent, Mosaic gave more to humanitarian projects in one month than in all of its history combined. We did more than build one house—we rediscovered who we were as a community of faith.

It was not long after when a devastating earthquake hit the small island of Haiti. The entire world seemed to stop for a moment with a global showing of empathy and sorrow. How could so poor a country withstand such a devastating catastrophe? Within days we could see the posture of Mosaic become more than evident. Teams began volunteering not only to give sacrificially but also to travel to Haiti immediately and work to bring relief. One of those teams was Kim's. In spite of the worst possible conditions, they were intent on bringing relief firsthand. Some members of our team have remained in Haiti when others in the world have since forgotten.

This is the barbarian way. It is the path we find ourselves on when we choose our most heroic lives. I know the term *barbarian* seems distinctly masculine, but bravery is not a gender. The reality is, women have given birth to every human being ever—and they also have been the conduit of much of the world's good. Truth be told, while men have held positions of power since the beginning of recorded time, they have rarely used that power to advance good in the world. Women, it seems, have always been more conscious of society. In underdeveloped countries, if you want to see a community turned around, you invest your economic development funds in the women. It should be the men, but time and time again we find that this is not the case. Men far too often squander the resources on their own short-term desires. Women will not only defer meeting their own needs but will focus their resources on their children, their community, and securing a better future.

Seeing this vision of the future, sacrificing to achieve it, and *unleashing* your own dreams and desires for the good of others—this is the core of the barbarian way. Just one step ahead of you, there is a beautiful and impactful life of servanthood, a life that advances the most good, and somehow, in some small way, a life that reveals the power of God through an unbridled, childlike faith. *Unleash it.*

When the idea for *The Barbarian Way* first hit me, I titled it *The Barbarian Way Out of Civilization.* The image I saw was a faith version of *The Truman Show*—a Christianity that had become civilized, domesticated, and complacent. All of us, it seems, are susceptible to choosing a life defined more by security and safety than faith and risk. I'm convinced that all of us struggle with the tension of wanting to live a life of unimaginable adventure and at the same time maintain a world that is fully under our control. The problem is that faith when fully ignited moves our lives entirely out of our control completely into the hands of God. I am convinced of this one thing—the life you long to live is not waiting in the future; it is waiting in the inner recesses of your soul. You don't need to go find faith; you need to unleash it. You don't need to go find life; you need to unleash it. In fact, everything that is good or beautiful and true that you will spend your entire life searching for is simply waiting to be set free through a life that follows Christ with reckless abandon.

The barbarian way is a journey that discovers the power of an untamed faith. And while this journey may genuinely be the narrow road that Jesus spoke of where very few enter in, what I do know is that if you choose this path, you will for the very first time live a life completely *unleashed*.

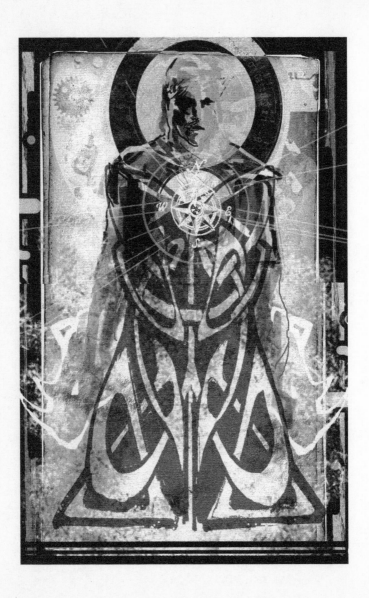

1

THE
BARBARIAN
INVASION

Now Jephthah the Gileadite was a mighty man of valor, but he was the son of a harlot; and Gilead begot Jephthah. Gilead's wife bore sons; and when his wife's sons grew up, they drove Jephthah out, and said to him, "You shall have no inheritance in our father's house, for you are the son of another woman." Then Jephthah fled from his brothers and dwelt in the land of Tob; and *worthless men banded together with Jephthah and went out raiding with him.*

It came to pass after a time that the people of Ammon made war against Israel. And so it was, when the people of Ammon made war against Israel, that the elders of Gilead went to get Jephthah from the land of Tob. Then they said to Jephthah, "Come and be our commander, that we may fight against the people of Ammon."

So Jephthah said to the elders of Gilead, "Did you not hate me, and expel me from my father's house? Why have you come to me now when you are in distress?"

And the elders of Gilead said to Jephthah, "That is why we have turned again to you now, that you may go with us and fight against the people of Ammon, and be our head over all the inhabitants of Gilead."

So Jephthah said to the elders of Gilead, "If you take me back home to fight against the people of Ammon, and the LORD delivers them to me, shall I be your head?"

And the elders of Gilead said to Jephthah, "The LORD will be a witness between us, if we do not do according to your words." Then Jephthah went with the elders of Gilead, and the people made him head and commander over them. (Judges 11:1–11 NKJV, italics added)

O n our way to Belfast, Northern Ireland, we made a stop in Paisley, Scotland. My wife, Kim, my twelve-year-old daughter, Mariah, and I were on a Hollywood version of a spiritual pilgrimage. (If you walk into our living room, you will find hanging as a centerpiece an exact replica of the sword that William Wallace made famous to the non-Scottish masses through Mel Gibson's *Braveheart*.) I was standing in the middle of the Paisley Abbey where Wallace was educated as a boy. I took my time as I looked reverently at the stained glass that remains a memorial to Wallace's heroics (he didn't look anything like Mel Gibson), yet it was a story about Robert the Bruce that struck me most and has stayed with me ever since.

Robert the Bruce was the Scottish noble whose character is most remembered for betraying Wallace, but he later rose up to lead Scotland to freedom after Wallace's execution. While we were standing in the abbey, Scottish pastor James Pettigrew shared a tale of Robert the Bruce that is a mixture of history and legend.

He died in 1329 at the age of fifty-four. Shortly before his death, Robert the Bruce requested that his heart be removed from his body and taken on crusade by a worthy knight. James Douglas, one of his closest friends, was at his bedside and took on the responsibility. The heart of Robert the Bruce was embalmed and placed in a small container that Douglas carried around his neck. In every battle that Douglas fought, he literally carried the heart of his king pressed against his chest.

In the early spring of 1330, Douglas sailed from Scotland to Granada, Spain, and engaged in a campaign against the

Moors. In an ill-fated battle, Douglas found himself surrounded, and in this situation death was both certain and imminent. In that moment Douglas reached for the heart strapped around his neck, flung the heart into the enemy's midst, and cried out, "Fight for the heart of your king!" One historian quoted Douglas as shouting, "Forward, brave heart, as ever thou were wont to do, and Douglas will follow his king's heart or die!" The motto of the Douglas clan to which the present duke belongs is even to this day simply, "Forward."

A TRIBE CALLED FORWARD

Although anyone who understands the heart of God knows that the Crusades were a tragic lesson in missing the point, the power of this story awakens within me a primal longing that I am convinced waits to be unleashed within everyone who is a follower of Jesus Christ. To belong to God is to belong to His heart. If we have responded to the call of Jesus to leave everything and follow Him, then there is a voice within us crying out, "Fight for the heart of your King!"

Yet Christianity over the past two thousand years has moved from a tribe of renegades to a religion of conformists. Those who choose to follow Jesus become participants in an insurrection. To claim we believe is simply not enough. The call of Jesus is one that demands action. Jesus began His public ministry with a simple invitation: "Come, follow Me." His closing instructions to His disciples can be summarized in one word, "Go!" A quick survey of the modern church would lead you to believe His invitation was "Come, and listen," and His closing mandate would be summarized in the one word "No!" The tribe of Jesus, above all people, should rightly carry the banner, "Forward."

I know the imagery of this story is nothing less than barbaric, but maybe that's the point. The invitation of Jesus is a revolutionary call to fight for the heart of humanity. We are called to an unconventional war using only the weapons of faith, hope, and love. Nevertheless, this war is no less dangerous than any war ever fought. And for those of us who embrace the cause of Christ, the cost to participate in the mission of God is nothing less than everything we are and everything we have.

Strangely enough, though, some who come to Jesus Christ

seem to immediately and fully embrace this barbarian way. They live their lives with every step moving forward and with every fiber of their being fighting for the heart of their King. Jesus Christ has become the all-consuming passion of their lives. They are not about religion or position. They have little patience for institutions or bureaucracies. Their lack of respect for tradition or ritual makes them seem uncivilized to those who love religion. When asked if they are Christians, their answer might surprisingly be no, they are passionate followers of Jesus Christ. They see Christianity as a world religion, in many ways no different from any other religious system. Whether Buddhism, Hinduism, Islam, or Christianity, they're not about religion; they're about advancing the revolution Jesus started two thousand years ago.

This is the simplicity of the barbarian way. If you are a follower of Christ, then you are called to fight for the heart of your King. It is a life fueled by passion—a passion for God and a passion for people. The psalmist tells us to delight ourselves in the Lord, and He will give us the desires of our hearts (Psalm 37:4). When Christianity becomes just another religion, it focuses on requirements. Just to keep people in line, we build our own Christian civilization and then demand that everyone who believes in Jesus become a good citizen.

It's hard to imagine that Jesus would endure the agony of the Cross just to keep us in line. Jesus began a revolution to secure our freedom. The new covenant that He established puts its trust not in the law, but in the transforming power of God's Spirit living within us. The revolution of the human heart would fuel the life and vitality of this movement. We would delight in God, and He would give us the desires of our hearts. With our hearts burning for God, we would move forward with the freedom to pursue the passions burning within us.

RAW LOVE

My daughter, Mariah, and I were eating Thai food in San Diego. We were getting some important dad-and-daughter time. There's nothing like one-on-one to create an environment for some real heart-to-heart conversation. After she reminded me that I was the only one between the two of us who liked Thai, she began to open her heart and bring me into her dreams.

"Daddy, one day I want to make a billion dollars, and I want to give it all away. I want to help the poor; I want to help the needy. I want to make a billion dollars, and I don't care if I have nothing, but I want to give it all to help people."

As I was listening to her dream, I thought, *I can fix this.* Because the dream was almost right.

But she kept saying, "I want to make a billion dollars and give it away and help the poor, and I don't care if I'm homeless or have nothing. I just want to give it away to help people."

I said, "Mariah, I want you to make a billion dollars and give to the poor and the needy, but it's not a good idea that you have nothing. Then you would be needy and somebody would have to take care of you and you wouldn't be responsible."

"I don't care if I don't have anything, Daddy," Mariah responded. "I just want to make a billion dollars and give it away. I don't care if I'm homeless. I don't care if I have nothing."

"But if you're homeless, our taxes would have to pay for you."

Looking at me as if to say, *Daddy, you just don't understand,* she continued, "I don't care if I have nothing. I just want to make a billion dollars and give it all away. I don't care if I have nothing."

I thought, *Okay, I'm not really helping here.* I was trying to help her understand that she needed to keep something, restructure it, and reinvest it so that she could make another billion and help another group of people. I just wasn't able to help her with her dream. And I thought, *A metaphor—that will help.*

"Honey, let's say you're a large tree bearing fruit for people to eat because they are hungry, and you want to give all your fruit away because you want to feed everyone, care for everyone. But because of that, you didn't care about your roots, and so you said, 'I'm going to uproot myself. Who cares about the soil and the water? I just want to bear all the fruit I can.' And then you will die. Then the next year you won't be able to bear fruit. It's better to take care of your roots, too, so that you can keep bearing fruit year after year after year."

She said, "Daddy, what in the world do roots have to do with this?"

I knew I wasn't making progress. We left the place and went to the car. I unlocked it, and she got into the car quickly. By the time I slid into the driver's seat, she was sobbing, and

I didn't know what was going on. I asked, "Mariah, are you okay?"

Just drenched in tears, she looked at me and said, "Daddy, I want to change the world, but you can't appreciate my dream. I want to change the world." She continued, "I didn't say I would be homeless; I said I didn't care if I became homeless. I want to change the world. Can't you just hear my dream?"

I realized that instead of nurturing and unleashing the dream being born out of her heart for God, I was domesticating her dream and trying to civilize her raw and untamed faith, which was ironic since I was so excited that this was her heart.

"Well, honey, I am excited about your dream," I said. "Don't you think that we were a small part of trying to nurture your heart to have that dream?"

She said, "Yeah, but I don't think you're getting it."

I said, "Well, I get it now. I get it now."

It took me a little while, but suddenly I saw it clearly. I was experiencing a barbarian invasion. Mariah's heart was beating to the rhythm of the heart of God. And her dreams were way too raw for me. I didn't see it initially, but I was trying to civilize her instead of unleashing the untamed faith within her. After all, I am her dad. It's okay if I live a life of irrational faith and breathtaking adventure. I want something different for her. I want her to have security and safety—you know, a predictable, boring, mundane life where I never have to worry about her again. In that moment I realized Mariah would have none of that. For her there is only one path. Even at twelve she has already committed to it. Be still my heart, but my daughter has chosen the barbarian way out of civilization. And it's for this simple reason that this book is dedicated to her.

OF WIND AND FIRE

Twenty-five years ago I was a part of the barbarian invasion. I knew little about God, but I wanted to know nothing else but God. I was overwhelmed that Someone as extraordinary as Jesus of Nazareth would have any interest or desire to embrace someone like me. Even before I knew what was written on the pages of the sacred text that we know as the Bible, I knew that I would give my heart fully to whatever I would learn was on God's heart. I was a follower of Jesus, and for me there was no turning back.

Over the years I have met perhaps thousands who have been a part of this barbarian invasion. From my brother, Alex, who swore allegiance to Christ, even though he had no idea that heaven existed; to my wife, Kim, who as a child growing up in a foster home cried out to Jesus that she would go anywhere He wanted and do anything He wanted her to do. In their unique voices they were committing to move forward and fight for the heart of their King.

Perhaps the tragedy of our time is that such an overwhelming number of us who declare Jesus as Lord have become domesticated—or, if you will, civilized. We have lost the simplicity of our early faith. Beyond that, we have lost the passion and power of that raw, untamed, and primal faith. Maybe John was alluding to that in the Apocalypse when he told the church of Ephesus that they had lost their first love (Revelation 2:1–4). God's command to Israel was simply, "Love the LORD your God with all your heart and with all your soul and with all your strength. These commandments that I give you today are to be upon your hearts" (Deuteronomy 6:5–6). And when Jesus was asked, "What is the greatest of all the commandments?" and "How do I inherit eternal life?" His answer was the same, except to add that we are to love our neighbor as ourselves (Mark 10:17–19; 12:28–31).

The barbarian way is about love, intimacy, passion, and sacrifice. Barbarians love to live and live to love. For them God is life, and their mission is to reconnect humanity to Him. Their passion is that each of us might live in intimate communion with Him who died for us. The barbarian way is a path of both spirit and truth. The soul of the barbarian is made alive by the presence of Jesus.

As John the Baptist reminded us, the evidence that Jesus is the Christ is that He baptizes us in both Spirit and fire. Barbarians are guided by the wind of God and ignited by the fire of God. The way of the barbarian can be found only by listening to the voice of the Spirit. The barbarian way can be known only by those who have the heart of God. The steps of the barbarian are guided by the footprints of Jesus. Barbarians see the invisible and hear the inaudible because their souls are alive to God.

If I know nothing else about you, if you are a follower of Jesus Christ, I know this without question: there is within you a raw and untamed faith waiting to be unleashed. When we come to the living God, He consumes who we are and gives us life that is fueled by His presence. You have been recreated to live in a raw and primal spirituality. Jesus came to ignite a fire within you that would consume you and ignite you. Jesus the King came to fight for your heart. If He has won your heart, then to follow your heart will always lead you to follow the heart of God. He will always lead you to advance forward behind enemy lines to win the hearts of those who do not yet know Him or love Him.

A FASHIONABLE FIGHT

One of my favorite characters in *Braveheart* was the Irish guy who joined William Wallace in his crusade. Remember him, the crazy guy who talked to God? Appropriately his name was Stephen. His most memorable quote was this: "The Almighty says this must be a fashionable fight. It draws the finest people." Of course, any civilized Christian knows why he's crazy. Every devout believer—in fact, any person of faith from any religious persuasion, whether Christian, Muslim, Buddhist, Hindu, or whatever—believes in prayer, but we all know prayer is supposed to be us talking to God. We get a little nervous when someone starts hearing from God.

What has the Almighty been saying to you lately? And when was the last time He called you to participate in a fashionable fight?

He's calling you to fight for the heart of your King. For some, doing this will be just way too barbaric, but for others, their only option will be to choose the barbarian way.

PRIMAL LEADERS

A barbarian invasion is taking place even right now. They are coming from the four corners of the earth and they are numbered among the unlikely. From the moment Jesus walked among us the invasion began. And just as with those who crossed paths with Him here on earth, those who are most religious will be most offended and indignant. Barbarians are not welcome among the civilized and are feared among the domesticated. The way of Jesus is far too savage for their sensibilities. The sacrifice of God's Son, the way of the Cross, the call to die to ourselves, all lack the dignity of a refined faith. Why insist on such a barbaric way? Why a reckless call to awaken the barbarian faith within us at the risk of endangering this great civilization we have come to know as Christianity?

Because Jesus did not suffer and die so that we could build for ourselves havens, but so that we might expand the kingdom of His love. Because invisible kingdoms are at war for the hearts and lives of every human being who walks on the face of this earth. And times of war require barbarians who are willing to risk life itself for the freedom of others. The irony, of course, is that barbarians are driven away in times of peace—they only disrupt our communities, traditions, and sensibilities. It is only in the most desperate of times—times of war or conflict—that these outcasts are welcomed or even invited to return.

Jephthah, the son of a harlot, was despised by his people and expelled from his tribe. Those who would later choose to join him were considered a band of worthless men, yet his story reminds us that the very ones who are unwanted and driven from among us are the ones we most need to lead in times of war. Barbarians can be counted as worthless when all is safe and secure, but dangerous times suddenly make them invaluable. We live in such times. And we are not ready for the great challenges set before us. We have not been prepared to take on any great quest, to battle any great enemy, or even to pursue the great dream for which we have been born. Instead,

Christianity has become our Shawshank, and our redemption will only come if we find the courage to escape the prison we have created for ourselves. Risking everything to live free is our only hope—humanity's only hope.

Jesus is being lost in a religion bearing His name. People are being lost because they cannot reconcile Jesus' association with Christianity. Christianity has become docile, domesticated, civilized. We have forgotten that there is a kingdom of darkness stealing the hopes and dreams and souls of a humanity without God. It is time to hear the barbarian call, to form a barbarian tribe, and to unleash the barbarian revolt. Let the invasion begin . . .

2

THE
BARBARIAN
CALL

After Jesus had finished instructing his twelve disciples, he went on from there to teach and preach in the towns of Galilee. When John heard in prison what Christ was doing, he sent his disciples to ask him, "Are you the one who was to come, or should we expect someone else?" Jesus replied, "Go back and report to John what you hear and see: The blind receive sight, the lame walk, those who have leprosy are cured, the deaf hear, the dead are raised, and the good news is preached to the poor. Blessed is the man who does not fall away on account of me." (Matthew 11:1–6)

If I'm right about this whole barbarian thing, then the women and men closest to God will most powerfully live out the raw and untamed spirit of the barbarian. We should ask, for instance: When Jesus walked among us, who did He choose to represent Him? Or maybe we should go back even a bit farther and ask, What kind of person did God choose to prepare the way for the coming of His Son? His name was John. We know him better as John the Baptist.

John the Baptist was a true barbarian. John was introduced to us with the full force of his personality:

In those days John the Baptist came, preaching in the Desert of Judea and saying, "Repent, for the kingdom of heaven is near." This is he who was spoken of through the prophet Isaiah:

"A voice of one calling in the desert,
'Prepare the way for the Lord,
    make straight paths for him.'"

John's clothes were made of camel's hair, and he had a leather belt around his waist. His food was locusts and wild honey. People went out to him from Jerusalem and all Judea and the whole region of the

Jordan. Confessing their sins, they were baptized by him in the Jordan River.

But when he saw many of the Pharisees and Sadducees coming to where he was baptizing, he said to them: "You brood of vipers! Who warned you to flee from the coming wrath? Produce fruit in keeping with repentance. And do not think you can say to yourselves, 'We have Abraham as our father.' I tell you that out of these stones God can raise up children for Abraham. The ax is already at the root of the trees, and every tree that does not produce good fruit will be cut down and thrown into the fire.

"I baptize you with water for repentance. But after me will come one who is more powerful than I, whose sandals I am not fit to carry. He will baptize you with the Holy Spirit and with fire. His winnowing fork is in his hand, and he will clear his threshing floor, gathering his wheat into the barn and burning up the chaff with unquenchable fire." (Matthew 3:1–12)

Several things about John stand out right away. He was an unusual dresser with strange eating habits. Just in case you're uncertain, wearing clothes made of camel's hair was not the height of fashion, even during the time of Jesus. We are told he ate locusts and wild honey. I suppose the wild honey was to help get the locusts down.

He was clearly not a fan of the established religious leaders. His nickname for the Pharisees and Sadducees, who were the pinnacle of the religious elite, was "brood of vipers." Nope, that was not a term of endearment. And I think it's important to note that his fire-and-brimstone message was entirely directed toward the religious, not the irreligious. He was a barbarian in the midst of civilization. And frankly the civilization made him sick. He had no patience for domesticated religionists who were drowning in their own self-righteousness.

Oh, and by the way, he had no formal education, no degrees. His occupation was prophet, and his mailing address was the wilderness. To say the very least, he was not the person whom anyone was expecting to prepare the way for the Messiah. John was the voice that proclaimed the coming of the Christ, and through his encounters with Jesus, we can rediscover the barbarian call.

BEYOND DOUBT

John sent his disciples to ask Jesus a question: "Are you the one who was to come, or should we expect someone else?" (Matthew 11:3). It was a fair question, wouldn't you think? In fact, it's a question that all of us should ask. If Jesus is not the One, we should not follow Him. But if He is the One, we should follow Him at all costs.

I myself asked this question about twenty years ago. I hope that you have asked this question. I always feel hopeful when a person who has been indifferent begins to ask this question about Jesus. Yet for John, this question seemed entirely out of place. How could John be uncertain whether Jesus was the One? Remember, Jesus and John were cousins. Mary and Elizabeth were pregnant with their sons at the very same time. In an extraordinary story recorded by Luke, we are told,

At that time Mary got ready and hurried to a town in the hill country of Judea, where she entered Zechariah's home and greeted Elizabeth. When Elizabeth heard Mary's greeting, the baby leaped in her womb, and Elizabeth was filled with the Holy Spirit. In a loud voice she exclaimed: "Blessed are you among women, and blessed is the child you will bear! But why am I so favored, that the mother of my Lord should come to me? As soon as the sound of your greeting reached my ears, the baby in my womb leaped for joy. Blessed is she who has believed that what the Lord has said to her will be accomplished!" (1:39–45)

Do you see it? When John was inside his mother's womb and Jesus was inside His mother's womb, John leaped. He recognized Jesus from the fetal position. I can only imagine a little voice emanating from Elizabeth's belly, asking, "Are You the One, or should we look for another?" In the womb, John knew, but then thirty years later he was uncertain?

And it seems that God was prepared to clarify in John's adulthood what he knew before he was born. In the first chapter of the gospel of John, John the Baptist was in the middle of a controversial conversation with the religious leaders (vv. 19–28). John was clear that his one mission was to prepare the way for the coming Messiah. It was his job to point others to

Him. And that was exactly what he did. It was never his intention to gather a following to himself. His ultimate desire for any of his disciples was that they would become devoted followers of the Messiah to come.

On one occasion the apostle John told us, "The next day John was there again with two of his disciples. When he saw Jesus passing by, he said, 'Look, the Lamb of God!' When the two disciples heard him say this, they followed Jesus" (John 1:35–37).

One of those two disciples was Andrew, who became one of the Twelve that we have come to know as the apostles. He was also Simon Peter's brother. Even so early in the process, John was clear about who Jesus was. He was absolutely certain about the identity of Jesus—so much so that he led his disciples to become Jesus' followers. Why at that point wasn't John running up to Jesus and saying, "Are You the One? All you Nazarenes look the same."

BEYOND QUESTION

In between these two encounters, we find why John was so certain. The gospel tells us,

The next day John saw Jesus coming toward him and said, "Look, the Lamb of God, who takes away the sin of the world! This is the one I meant when I said, 'A man who comes after me has surpassed me because he was before me.' I myself did not know him, but the reason I came baptizing with water was that he might be revealed to Israel."

Then John gave this testimony: "I saw the Spirit come down from heaven as a dove and remain on him. I would not have known him, except that the one who sent me to baptize with water told me, 'The man on whom you see the Spirit come down and remain is he who will baptize with the Holy Spirit.' I have seen and I testify that this is the Son of God." (John 1:29–34)

John confessed that he was uncertain about whether Jesus was really the One. But His baptism removed all doubt. Matthew told us that in the moment John baptized Jesus, the heavens were opened, and John saw the Spirit of God descending on Jesus like a dove and lighting on Him. And he also heard a voice from heaven declare, "This is my Son, whom I love; with him I am well pleased" (Matthew 3:16–17).

In other words, by that time John was absolutely clear about one thing: Jesus was the One. I guarantee you, no one else whom John baptized had that kind of drama surrounding the event. A voice coming out of the heavens, and what by today's standards would be amazing special effects, would be enough to convince even the most skeptical of us. John was neither unclear nor uncertain, and in his barbaric rawness the untamed prophet defied anyone who would deny the legitimacy of Jesus.

With that knowledge John declared his subservience to the purpose and person of Jesus the Christ. Without shame or ambiguity he would declare to those who questioned him, "I baptize with water . . . but among you stands one you do not know. He is the one who comes after me, the thongs of whose sandals I am not worthy to untie" (John 1:26–27).

So what in the world was John thinking then? How could he send his disciples with a question like that? How could he be gripped with so much doubt that he would risk spreading it to his disciples? All who were close to him had heard him declare the supremacy of Jesus. All of them had to be affected by the strength of his confidence in who Jesus was. Why would he ask Jesus, "Are you the one who was to come, or should we expect someone else?" (Matthew 11:3).

HEAD GAMES

We don't have to go far to find the reason for John's confusion. Just before Matthew recorded John's question, he let us know what prompted John's crisis of faith. John was in prison. Herod arrested John and put him in prison on account of Herodias. Herodias was the wife of his brother Philip, and Herod was having an affair with her. In his expectedly barbaric way, John called it for what it was, refusing to placate Herod or cower to Herod's power. Herod wanted to kill John, but he feared the reaction of the people. The people loved John because they considered him a prophet from God.

Anyway, one day it was Herod's birthday, and the daughter of Herodias danced for him. Herod was so pleased (I think this alludes to the dark and evil kind of pleased) that he made an oath to give her whatever she asked. In a plot between Herodias and her daughter, they asked for John the Baptist's head on a platter. Though the king was distressed for political reasons, he granted what they asked (Matthew 14:1–12). That was the backdrop of John's dilemma.

John was living between prison and platter when he sent the message to Jesus. Shouldn't he expect Jesus to drop everything and come to his aid? After all, he had always been there for Jesus. Where was He when John needed Him? Was He unaware that John needed help? Was He indifferent to John's dilemma? Or was He simply not the Messiah as John had always believed?

When Jesus received the inquiry from John's disciples, He gave an impressive response: "Go back and report to John what you hear and see: The blind receive sight, the lame walk, those who have leprosy are cured, the deaf hear, the dead are raised, and the good news is preached to the poor. Blessed is the man who does not fall away on account of me" (Matthew 11:4–6).

At first glance you would think Jesus was trying to inspire John. Something like, "Don't sweat it, John. I'm doing everything that you would expect of a Messiah." You have to admit it's a pretty impressive résumé—the blind seeing, the lame walking, people with leprosy being cured, the deaf hearing, even the dead being raised, and to top it all off, the good news being preached to the poor. How do you argue with that? You just expect John to be overwhelmed with joy, come back to his senses, and wonder how he could ever have questioned whether Jesus was the One.

Except for one problem: John already knew all of that. In fact, Matthew told us that was a part of the problem: "When John heard in prison what Christ was doing, he sent his disciples to ask him . . ." (11:2–3). Well, you know the question. The amazing and inspiring work of Jesus didn't eliminate John's doubts; it actually fueled them.

Talk about a dilemma. Why would Jesus' doing so much good jeopardize John's faith? How could the very things that Jesus was doing to help others cause John to lose heart? When we look at Jesus' response to John, we see one line that just doesn't fit. After He reinforced all of the evidence that He was the Messiah, retelling His miraculous work among the people, He closed with this seemingly disconnected thought: "Blessed is the man who does not fall away on account of me."

Why would Jesus add that? Why would He even consider the thought that someone might fall away with so much good happening? I can't imagine anyone coming up to me and saying, "Too many blind people are regaining their sight.

I'm having a crisis of faith." Or someone confronting me with, "If one more person who is paralyzed rises and walks, I'm out of here." Miracles are rarely followed by a flood of recanting. Why would Jesus feel He needed to exhort John that "after all this good has been confirmed to you, you will be blessed if you do not fall away on account of Me"?

What Jesus was saying to John has been far too barbaric for us to keep in the mainstream of the Christian faith. Jesus was saying to him, "John, I'm not coming through for you. I'm not getting you out of prison. I'm not sparing your life. Yes, I have done all this and more for others, but the path I choose for you is different from theirs. You'll be blessed, John, if this does not cause you to fall away."

If that were not bad enough, we find the dissonance of this reality accentuated in one verse. In his opening chapter, Mark stated, "After John was put in prison, Jesus went into Galilee, proclaiming the good news of God" (1:14).

What exactly, one might ask, was the good news for John? Jesus knew all along that John had been imprisoned. He very well knew the fate that John would face. Even then Jesus understood His purpose was to save us not from pain and suffering, but from meaninglessness. For Jesus, John was exactly where he needed to be, fulfilling God's purpose for his life. Why would He save John from that? In that same passage Jesus explained, "The time has come . . . The kingdom of God is near. Repent and believe the good news!" (Mark 1:15).

A DANGEROUS INVITATION

So what is this good news? The refined and civilized version goes something like this: Jesus died and rose from the dead so that you can live a life of endless comfort, security, and indulgence. But really this is a bit too developed. Usually it's more like this: if you'll simply confess that you're a sinner and believe in Jesus, you'll be saved from the torment of eternal hellfire, then go to heaven when you die. Either case results in our domestication. One holds out for life to begin in eternity, and the other makes a mockery out of life.

The call of Jesus is far more barbaric than either of these. It is a call to live in this world as citizens of an entirely different kingdom. In its primitive state the good news could never be separated from the invitation of Jesus to "come, follow Me." He never lied about the danger or cost associated with becoming His follower. He told them up front, "I am sending you out like sheep among wolves. Therefore be as shrewd as snakes and as innocent as doves" (Matthew 10:16).

One danger of civilized faith is that we become so domesticated, we begin to live as shrewd as the dove. We are blind to the spiritual nature of life and the unseen reality in which we reside. Another danger is that we become as innocent as snakes. For far too long, sincere followers of Christ have had to live with the consequences of those who use religion to manipulate others and camouflage hypocrisy. Jesus made clear to those who were choosing to be His disciples what kind of leader He was and what kind of followers would be required.

When Jesus asked Peter, "Who do you say I am?" Peter answered, "The Christ of God." Jesus went on to tell him,

"The Son of Man must suffer many things and be rejected by the elders, chief priests and teachers of the law, and he must be killed and on the third day be raised to life." Then he said to them all: "If anyone would come after me, he must deny himself and take up his cross daily and follow me. For whoever wants to save his life will lose it, but whoever loses his life for me will save it. What good is it for a man to gain

the whole world, and yet lose or forfeit his very self?"
(Luke 9:20–25)

THE ROAD LESS TRAVELED

There was no pristine call to a proper religion. It was a barbaric call to a barbarian way. Peter understood that and struggled to live up to it. Jesus' words about love ignited the primal fires within Peter's faith. Longing to follow Jesus even to His death, he declared to Jesus, "Lord, why can't I follow You now? I will lay down my life for You."

Jesus' simple response was, "Will you really lay down your life for Me? I tell you the truth, before the rooster crows you will disown Me three times." (See Matthew 26:31–35.)

Yes, Peter failed in his endeavor, but he understood what Jesus was asking for. Love and sacrifice were inseparable. The barbarian way is not about violence fueled by vengeance and hatred. The barbarian way is about love expressed through sacrifice and servanthood.

After Jesus' death and resurrection, Peter and Jesus had another conversation about love and sacrifice. Three times Jesus asked Peter if he loved Him. And each time Peter responded by adamantly declaring his love. In fact, the Scriptures tell us that Peter was hurt because Jesus asked him a third time, "Do you love Me?" Peter's response was, "Lord, You know all things. You know that I love You."

Ready to move the conversation to a deeper level, Peter found himself being called to the barbarian way. Jesus said to him, "'I tell you the truth, when you were younger you dressed yourself and went where you wanted; but when you are old you will stretch out your hands, and someone else will dress you and lead you where you do not want to go.' Jesus said this to indicate the kind of death by which Peter would glorify God. Then he said to him, 'Follow me!'" (John 21:17–19).

Jesus had only one invitation for Peter, only one course set for him, only one path for him to choose if he were to journey with Christ—and that was the way of the barbarian. Jesus never watered down the cost of following Him in hopes that Peter would then choose to follow. If Peter chose the path with Christ, it would mean for him that one day he would be taken against his will and dragged off to be killed. If he wanted to live a life of love and allegiance to the Christ, it would cost him his life. We, too, are called to a path filled with uncertainty, mystery, and risk.

So how did Peter respond? He turned and made John the focus of the conversation: "Peter turned and saw that the disciple whom Jesus loved was following them. (This was the one who had leaned back against Jesus at the supper and had said, 'Lord, who is going to betray you?') When Peter saw him, he asked, 'Lord, what about him?'" (John 21:20–21).

I know exactly what Peter was doing. He was thinking, *If I'm going to die, I want to make sure everyone else has to die, especially him. After all, if the barbarian call is for all of us, wouldn't it come out the same for all of us? Wouldn't all of us have to suffer hardship and die a brutal death?* But it just doesn't work that way.

Jesus answered him, "If I want him to remain alive until I return, what is that to you? You must follow me" (John 21:22).

This is the sticky part of the barbarian call. It's not fair or equitable. When you hear the call, when you follow the call, you must recognize that it is a life-and-death proposition. When you understand what Jesus means when He says that you must follow Him, you finally realize that this is not a cattle call. He is not calling you to the same life that everyone else will live. He's not even calling you to the same path that every follower of Christ will walk. Your life is unique before God, and your path is yours and yours alone. Where God will choose to lead you and how God chooses to use your life cannot be predicted by how God has worked in the lives of others before you. Jesus' response to Peter was as straight-forward as it could possibly get: "If I want John to live and you to die, what is that to you? Your part is to follow Me. My part is to lead the way."

IT'S A RISKY BUSINESS

Christianity as a civilized religion claims to have a group plan negotiated with God. Everybody gets the same package. And of course, the package is always the premium plan—get rich, get comfortable, get secure, get safe, get well when you get God. Everybody gets the John plan; nobody gets the Peter package. The result and proof of faith are that you get to live a life without risk, which is ironic when you realize that for the early church, faith was a risky business.

Hebrews 11 has become known as the "hall of faith." It begins with the declaration "Now faith is being sure of what we hope for and certain of what we do not see. This is what the ancients were commended for" (vv. 1–2).

Throughout the chapter, the writer challenges us with the power and vitality of ancient faith. He points to individuals such as Abel, Enoch, Noah, Abraham, Joseph, and Moses. He even refers to some surprising faith heroes such as Rahab and Samson. In summarizing the exploits of this extraordinary list, the writer explains their qualifications by telling us, "Who through faith conquered kingdoms, administered justice, and gained what was promised; who shut the mouths of lions, quenched the fury of the flames, and escaped the edge of the sword; whose weakness was turned to strength; and who became powerful in battle and routed foreign armies. Women received back their dead, raised to life again" (Hebrews 11:33–35).

This is the kind of stuff that all of us think of when we think of women and men of faith. When we live by faith, we don't die by the sword. When we live by faith, every battle is won and every enemy conquered. When we live by faith, lions go hungry, executioners become unemployed, and the Grim Reaper's prospects look grim.

But faith doesn't stop here. Oh, how I wish it did. It would make life so much easier. But it really only begins here. This short list of the faithful (and I want to emphasize *short*) is pointing us not to the rule, but to the exception to the rule. These men and women are listed exactly because their lives were so extraordinary and the results were so unusual. I'm not saying that God doesn't work like this anymore. What I am saying is that God is just getting started. He has far deeper and more profound work to do in and through us.

Any understanding of faith that is genuinely rooted in the Scriptures must always make room for the "others." Who are the others? We don't exactly know. We just know how faith worked out in their lives. After all, isn't that what Jesus was preparing us for? Speaking to His disciples, Jesus said, "If the world hates you, keep in mind that it hated me first . . . 'No servant is greater than his master.' If they persecuted me, they will persecute you also" (John 15:18–20). Peter continued this theme by reminding us: "Do not be surprised at the painful trial you are suffering, as though something strange were happening to you. But rejoice that you participate in the sufferings of Christ" (1 Peter 4:12–13).

Hebrews continues describing the heroes of faith in verse 35. After telling us that women received back their dead raised to life again, the writer states,

Others were tortured and refused to be released, so that they might gain a better resurrection. Some faced jeers and flogging, while still others were chained and put in prison. They were stoned; they were sawed in two; they were put to death by the sword. They went about in sheepskins and goatskins, destitute, persecuted and mistreated—the world was not worthy of them. They wandered in deserts and mountains, and in caves and holes in the ground. These were all commended for their faith, yet none of them received what had been promised. God had planned something better for us so that only together with us would they be made perfect. (Hebrews 11:35–40)

The others experienced a different result of faith. To say the very least, their lives were far less desirable than the lives of those we've come to know from biblical fame. Yet their lives were no less expressions of a life well lived and fully lived in the presence and power of God than those we aspire to emulate. All were commended for their faith. Although the first group of the faithful have names that will be known throughout history, the others remain nameless. That is not because they lived a life of lesser faith, but because there were so many more of them.

All of them chose and walked the barbarian way, and they were blessed because they did not fall away on account of Jesus. They trusted Jesus with their lives, and they lost their lives on the journey. If you could interview any one of them, however, each would insist that even in the midst of the suffering and hardship, he was most fully alive. They were not disappointed in God because they did not misunderstand who He was. They understood His call, and they chose it willingly. John the Baptist would join their number. Some barbarians survive the night in the lion's den; others experience their darkest night and wake in eternity.

CONFESSIONS OF A DANGEROUS MIND

Mariah and I were in San Diego, and after an event, I had a mildly hostile encounter. The experience somewhat unnerved her. But more than anything else, it seemed to pique her curiosity. She asked, "You make a lot of people mad, don't you, Dad?"

"Sometimes."

Pressing further, she asked, "Has anyone ever tried to hurt you?"

"Yes."

"Has anyone ever tried to kill you?"

I said, "Sort of."

"Tell me," she insisted with as much excitement as I've seen in a father-daughter conversation.

So I described an encounter I wrote about in *An Unstoppable Force*. I told her there was an ex-convict who let me know while he was in prison that as soon as he was released, he was going to bring my life to a close. Instead of waiting for him when he hit the streets, I found him in the projects. Knowing I had Mariah captivated, I did everything I could to heighten the danger and mystery of the moment. I paused right after describing the dingy room in which only the two of us stood face-to-face—William holding open the same blade with which he had slit another man's throat; me with nowhere to go.

Before I could go on, Mariah couldn't keep it in. With panic in her eyes she blurted out, "Did he kill you?"

It may seem cruel, but I refused to tell her. It's possible

that even to this day, my daughter thinks her father is dead. (I need to add that Mariah gives me permission to share this story with you on the condition that I clearly communicate to you that she was very tired that night.)

The barbarian understands the story we're in differently from the one who is civilized. Although Mariah should have known the outcome of my story, in some ways she has a better understanding of reality than some of us. We've been taught that every story Jesus writes with our lives ends with "and they lived happily ever after." Mariah knows better. She knows that good people die, that men and women who make heroic choices do not always live to tell their own tales. Sometimes another must tell the stories of their lives, recall the memory of their courage. The civilized view of Jesus is that He always comes through for us. Like Superman, He always shows up just in time to protect us and save us from disaster. His purpose is to ensure our safety, our convenience, and our comfort.

For years I have made it my mission to destroy the influence of the Christian cliché "The safest place to be is in the center of the will of God," but just this past week my wife, Kim, introduced me to one of the earlier uses of this adage.

It's found in the diary of Corrie ten Boom. Corrie's sister, Betsie, was encouraging her with this hope. I've always had a great disdain for this statement, but I have to admit this particular context shows me how far we've strayed from how it must have been understood. For Corrie and Betsie, the promise of safety in the center of God's will was fleshed out in concentration camps during the Nazi holocaust of the Jews. And although Corrie lived to tell the story, Betsie died in the midst of it.

Clearly neither of them concluded that this expression conveyed a belief that God would keep them from suffering hardship and even death. Betsie's statement was a declaration that to walk in the character of Christ is always the right choice, regardless of outcome or consequence. We have somehow perverted this more primal understanding to a far more civilized one. Instead of finding confidence to live as we should regardless of our circumstances, we have used it as justification to choose the path of least resistance, least difficulty, least sacrifice. Instead of concluding it is best to be wherever God wants us to be, we have decided that wherever it is best for us to be is where God wants us. Actually, God's will for us is less about our comfort than it is about our contribution.

God would never choose for us safety at the cost of significance. God created you so that your life would count, not so that you could count the days of your life.

HIGH-RISK VENTURES

Do you think John the Baptist felt safe being in the center of the will of God while Jesus was busy proclaiming the good news to others, yet leaving him in prison? And when John was about to lose his head over his allegiance to the Son of God, do you think he was feeling overwhelmed by God's protecting hand?

If the safest place to be is in the center of the will of God, then how do you explain the life and ministry of Stephen—one sermon and then stoned to death? Was he really that bad? If the safest place to be is in the center of the will of God, then why is it that the biblical word for *witness* is actually the word for *martyr*?

If the safest place to be is in the center of the will of God, then how do you explain the experience of Paul? Paul walked with God, and certainly whatever the center of the will of God looks like, Paul had to have visited there at least a few times in his life. His journals, however, described not a life filled with safety and certainty, but a life of adventure and danger. Paul said of his journeys:

> I have . . . been in prison more frequently, been flogged more severely, been exposed to death again and again. Five times I received from the Jews the forty lashes minus one. Three times I was beaten with rods, once I was stoned, three times I was shipwrecked, I spent a night and a day in the open sea, I have been constantly on the move. I have been in danger from rivers, in danger from bandits, in danger from my own countrymen, in danger from Gentiles; in danger in the city, in danger in the country, in danger at sea; and in danger from false brothers. I have labored and toiled and have often gone without sleep; I have known hunger and thirst and have often gone without food; I have been cold and naked. (2 Corinthians 11:23–27)

Somebody forgot to tell Paul how safe the center of God's will was. Having been given that insight, wouldn't he have known to redirect his life? Danger would have been his first clue that he was out of God's will—unless, of course, he was a barbarian. Paul had heard the barbarian call. He knew exactly who Jesus was and the life to which he had been called. Paul had been a religionist. He had learned the art of condemning others while hiding behind his pompous self-righteousness—which, by the way, is one of the great dangers of religion.

There may not be a more dangerous weapon for violence or oppression than religion. It seems counterintuitive, but when human beings create religions, we use them to control others through their guilt and shame. True religion always moves us to serve others and to give our lives to see those oppressed find freedom. Paul persecuted followers of Christ and even instigated their deaths, but then he risked his own life so that others might live. He once personified the very worst that happens when a religion becomes civilized. It moves away from God and oppresses humanity in God's name. Paul was once consumed by religion, but then he was transformed by the living presence of God Himself.

We, too, must find the barbarian way out of civilization. How have we come to this sanitized view of the faith to which

Jesus calls us? Somewhere along the way the movement of Jesus Christ became civilized as Christianity. We created a religion using the name of Jesus Christ and convinced ourselves that God's optimal desire for our lives was to insulate us in a spiritual bubble where we risk nothing, sacrifice nothing, lose nothing, worry about nothing. Yet Jesus' death wasn't to free us from dying, but to free us from the fear of death. Jesus came to liberate us so that we could die up front and then live. Jesus Christ wants to take us to places where only dead men and women can go.

I wonder how many of us have lost our barbarian way and have become embittered with God, confused in our faith because God doesn't come through the way we think He should. Is it possible that the transforming power of the church has been lost because we keep inviting people to step into the comfort, safety, and security of Jesus Christ? We've created a religious culture in which—even though we're the most blessed society in the history of the planet—our best-selling literature still focuses on how we can be more blessed. Maybe we need to step way back to the beginning of this movement.

The original call of Jesus was so simple, so clean, so clear:

"Follow Me." He wants us to surrender our lives to Him and follow Him into the unknown. And if it means a life of suffering, hardship, and disappointment, it will be worth it because following Jesus Christ is more powerful and more fulfilling than living with everything in the world minus Him. Have we forgotten this? Have we become so refined and so civilized that the benefits of our faith have become more precious and more valuable to us than the Benefactor of our faith?

I wonder how many of us are in that place of John the Baptist, at that crucible where God is asking, "Are you willing to lose everything on My behalf to gain everything I desire for you? Rather than living a long life, are you willing to live a life worth living?"

YOU FIRST

The Church Communication Network sent me an invitation to do a session on leadership at one of their national conferences. I had actually been unaware that training was available through this satellite system known as CCN. I had been asked to do a session where I would follow one of the most credible experts on church leadership. I was honored to get to do something in partnership with the caliber of leaders that were involved. I was both excited and nervous as I prepared to follow the main speaker. Somewhere in his lecture he started to say something that totally threw me. Point-blank he instructed, "Don't be an innovator; be an early adopter."

Hearing that created a crisis for me since I place an extremely high value on innovation. At Mosaic, the community where I serve as lead pastor in Los Angeles, we don't describe ourselves as a modern church or a postmodern church, a contemporary church or an emerging church. The only description I use is that we're an experimental church. We volunteered to be God's R&D Department. Anything He wants to do that other churches do not want to do or are unwilling to do, we'd like to take on. A part of our ethos (the spirit of our congregational culture) is a value for risk, sacrifice, and creativity.

The speaker went on to explain that the innovator is the guy who eats the poisonous mushroom and dies. The early adopter is the guy right next to him, who doesn't have to eat it. He can learn from the innovator's misfortune. Made perfect sense to me. That's why he's the man. Curious to me was my perception that he had pretty much been an innovator, the kind of guy who had eaten some pretty bad mushrooms and just happened to live to tell about it.

Before I knew it, it was my turn. Whatever I had planned to talk about was irrelevant to what was banging around in my head. *Should I stop being an innovator? Was the wise choice to become an early adopter?* But my mind wouldn't stop there. *What happened if everyone became an early adopter? Who would be the innovator? If no one ate the mushroom, how would we ever know which ones are safe? Without innovators, who could we depend on to die?*

With all this running through my brain, I let my talk go where the lecture and perhaps God's Spirit guided me. After thanking him for his amazing contribution to the body of Christ and for mentoring me through his books and ministry, I went on to thank him for a new metaphor for my life. I am a mushroom eater.

I understand the risks. Perhaps more than ever before, the implications are clear—any day now might be my last supper. But without risking the poisonous mushroom, we never would have discovered the joys of portobellos. In a short time I gave this a lot of thought: *Why did that guy eat that first poisonous mushroom?* Which led me to other profound questions: *What could possibly have motivated someone to eat a sea cucumber or a jellyfish? What exactly drove that first consumer to eat a raw oyster or to decide that snails were for more than stepping on?*

My conclusion was simple: they were hungry, maybe even starving. If you're trapped at sea long enough, maybe you begin to wonder if the same jellyfish that stung you could also satisfy you. I could see a father with starving children boil up a pot of snails, call them escargot, and begin dinner by saying, "Look, children, we're rich and sophisticated." Before aristocracy dubbed fish eggs "caviar," some mother stretching the catch of the day to feed her entire family simply called it "dinner."

Innovation is a life skill. When we're surrounded by civilization, innovation tends to be motivated by boredom. When we are barbarians trying to reach barbarians, innovation is motivated by love. Barbarians are a people of the earth. We know how to survive in the wild. We understand that whoever walks in front walks closest to death, but even this knowledge does not slow us down.

The barbarian call is just this simple: we are called to be mushroom eaters. A world without God cannot wait for us to choose the safe path. If we wait for someone else to take the risk, we risk that no one will ever act and that nothing will ever be accomplished. John the Baptist was a mushroom eater, and it cost him his life. Jesus, too, was a mushroom eater, and He found Himself nailed to a tree. Neither man saw his thirty-fifth birthday. Both of them point to the barbarian way.

CALLED OUT

If you don't like the idea of being an innovator, that's fine. Just do whatever Jesus calls you to do the moment it is clear to you. Do not procrastinate; do not hesitate; do not deviate from whatever course of action He calls you to. But I want to warn you, the closer you walk with Christ, the greater the faith required. The more you trust Him, the more you'll risk on His behalf. The more you love Him, the more you will love others. If you genuinely embrace His sacrifice, you will joyfully embrace a sacrificial life. Your expectations of Jesus will change as your intimacy with Him deepens. When you begin to follow passionately after Jesus, you will inadvertently find yourself innovating. After all, Jesus is transforming lives, writing history, creating the future, and unleashing the kingdom of God. If you plan to keep step with Jesus the Pioneer, you better expect some changes.

Our civilized faith demands caviar and escargot; our barbaric faith accepts that we might have to eat fish eggs and snails. We look to Jesus not to fulfill our shallow longings or to provide for us creature comforts. We look to Him to lead us where He needs us most and where we can accomplish the most good.

Barbarians hear a call different from that of civilized Christians. We understand clearly that we follow the God who chose the way of the Cross. If Jesus would not avoid the "place of the skull," then we should not be surprised where He might lead us. If even He found Himself sweating blood at Gethsemane, then we should be certain we will stand at crisis moments where all we can do after asking for relief is declare, "Not my will, but Yours." In those moments you may find very few who stand by you to provide you comfort and strength, and strangely enough, you may find far too many trying to reason with you that God would never require so much of anyone. Yet even with all the noise pounding inside your head, you will still clearly hear the voice of Christ and His barbarian call if you listen carefully enough.

3

THE
BARBARIAN
TRIBE

As John's disciples were leaving, Jesus began to speak to the crowd about John: "What did you go out into the desert to see? A reed swayed by the wind? If not, what did you go out to see? A man dressed in fine clothes? No, those who wear fine clothes are in kings' palaces. Then what did you go out to see? A prophet? Yes, I tell you, and more than a prophet. This is the one about whom it is written: 'I will send my messenger ahead of you, who will prepare your way before you.' I tell you the truth: Among those born of women there has not risen anyone greater than John the Baptist; yet he who is least in the kingdom of heaven is greater than he." (Matthew 11:7–11)

Although John was confused about Jesus, Jesus was not confused about John. Jesus knew that everyone else was confused about John. John lacked religious pedigree, yet he clearly spoke with spiritual power. At the same time he didn't look anything like a priest or a teacher of the law. To put it bluntly, John was just plain weird. Not what you would expect when you were looking for a spiritual leader. John's faith was raw and untamed. There was nothing civilized about him.

And Jesus seemed to be either mocking or rebuking them for expecting to find someone different. If you were looking for a reed swayed by the wind (someone easily molded by the expectations of the civilized) or a man dressed in fine clothes (someone who lives to impress the political or religious elite), you were looking in the wrong place. But if you went out to see a prophet, John was your man. And he was more than a prophet. He was the one whom God chose to prepare the way for the coming of His Son. Of all the men born of women—and that pretty much covers everybody but Adam—John was the greatest. Jesus, by the way, was born of God. The assumption was that for such a job, God would choose someone with polish and refinement.

Jesus wanted to make clear that the greater the kingdom responsibility, the more a barbarian is required. But then He added something that opened up a floodgate of possibilities for the rest of us. Jesus said, "Yet he who is least in the kingdom of heaven is greater than he" (Matthew 11:11).

That means great opportunities are yet available for the rest of us. Jesus expected that John would be joined by a barbarian tribe to follow. Jesus lived in a time when Judaism had been domesticated, institutionalized, and civilized; it was only a hollow shell of what God intended. John didn't fit into the organized religion of his time because God didn't fit either. Jesus Himself, the Messiah of Israel, remained an outsider even to His death.

Jesus described this barbarian controversy as He pointed out how domesticated they had become:

To what can I compare this generation? They are like children sitting in the marketplaces and calling out to others:

"We played the flute for you, and you did not dance; we sang a dirge, and you did not mourn."

For John came neither eating nor drinking, and they say, "He has a demon." The Son of Man came eating and drinking, and they say, "Here is a glutton and a drunkard, a friend of tax collectors and 'sinners.'" (Matthew 11:16–19)

In other words, no matter what a person who is genuinely following God does, you find a reason to disdain him. Jesus concluded, "But wisdom is proved right by her actions."

Jesus was making clear that being a disciple was never intended to be the equivalent of being molded into a stereotype. Jesus and John were considered barbarians, even though they expressed themselves in different ways. But at the core they were the same. They lived and moved in the mystical. That is, they had a unique and transcendent connection to the Creator of the universe. Guided by the voice of God, they cared little how others perceived that. What was invisible to others was clear to them. Their lives could not be explained apart from God.

While He walked among us, Jesus tried to explain this to us. He told us—as if we should understand without difficulty—that He spoke only what He heard the Father saying and did only what He saw the Father doing. He called His disciples to make this their pattern for living.

Somehow Christianity has become a nonmystical religion. It's about a reasonable faith. If we believe the right things, then we are orthodox. Frankly whether we ever actually connect to God or experience His undeniable presence has become incidental, if not irrelevant. We have become believers rather than experiencers. To know God in the Scriptures always went beyond information to intimacy. We may find ourselves uncomfortable with this reality, but the faith of the Scriptures is a mystical faith. It leads us beyond the material world into an invisible reality. We become connected to the God of eternity. Who you are at the core is spirit. God is Spirit. To walk with God is to journey in the spiritual realm.

MYSTIC WARRIORS

Our spiritual heritage is filled with people like Enoch, who walked with God for three hundred years, and "then he was no more, because God took him away" (Genesis 5:21–24). And Abram, whose spiritual journey began with the voice of God calling him to a life of reckless abandon: "Leave your country, your people and your father's household and go to the land I will show you" (Genesis 12:1). "So Abram left, as the LORD had told him" (Genesis 12:4). And then there was Samuel, who heard a voice in the night. His story began, "In those days the word of the LORD was rare; there were not many visions . . . Then the LORD called Samuel" (1 Samuel 3:1, 10). Three times he heard the voice in the night. And following Eli the high priest's instruction, Samuel responded, "Speak, for your servant is listening." And, of course, who can forget Elijah, running from the evil Queen Jezebel and hiding in a cave in a mountain? The Lord commanded him to

"go out and stand on the mountain in the presence of the LORD, for the LORD, is about to pass by." Then a great and powerful wind tore the mountains apart and shattered the rocks before the LORD, but the LORD was not in the wind. After the wind there was an earthquake, but the LORD was not in the earthquake. After the earthquake came a fire, but the LORD was not in the fire. And after the fire came a gentle whisper. When Elijah heard it, he pulled his cloak over his face and went out and stood at the mouth of the cave. Then a voice said to him, "What are you doing here, Elijah?" (1 Kings 19:11–13)

These people, and many others like them, were the barbarian tribe. Their stories began and ended with God. They were mystical warriors called out to advance the cause of the Creator of the universe.

Every one of us who is a follower of Jesus Christ is called to join the same tribe, to live the same way. For the early disciples, Jesus was right there for them to watch and hear. For the rest of us, we have to learn how to see the invisible and hear the inaudible. We are called to join the barbarian tribe and to embrace our call as mystical warriors. Although you can learn important things about God from others, in the end to know the barbarian way you must receive your instructions from God Himself. If this isn't enough to drive you crazy, I don't know what is. Which I guess leads me to the point: there's a level of insanity that comes with the barbarian way.

Thoreau talked about individuals who march to the beat of a different drummer. Barbarians have never met the drummer. In the civilized view of discipleship, everything and everyone moves toward the center. Discipleship is translated into standardizing everyone into the same pattern. We have equated the promise that we would be conformed into the image of Christ with a belief that all of us will be the same. Discipleship has become the mechanism for uniformity rather than uniqueness.

Yet if we learn anything about God through John, it is that God has no problem with spiritual eccentrics. The point, of course, is not that God makes us mentally or emotionally imbalanced, but that He makes us passionately and spiritually unbalanced. God steers us in the direction of His kingdom, His purpose, His passions. His desire is not to conform us, but to transform us. Not to make us compliant, but to make us creative. His intent is never to domesticate us, but to liberate us.

Is it possible that God is the cause of such abnormality? How many of us would actually expect the person who came to prepare the way for Christ to present himself wearing animal skins, eating locusts, and wandering around in the desert? If he lived today, he would be medicated and diagnosed bipolar. He would be one more certified lunatic. And that's just what would happen if the church were in charge of his diagnosis. Most of us would think that John was out of his mind.

Confronted by John, we have to stop and ask ourselves: "If this is what the person looked like who prepared the way for Jesus, then what should a disciple of Jesus Christ look like who comes after Jesus? How is it possible that, for many of us, being a good Christian is really nothing more than being a good person?" The entire focus of our faith has been the elimination of sin, which is important but inadequate, rather than the unleashing of a unique, original, extraordinary, wonderfully untamed faith.

You can't escape that John acted like a madman. God drove him out of his mind. The path to which God called him put him out of step with the cultural rhythm. Paul struggled with the same dilemma. He told us that if his only concern were for God, he would be out of his mind. But for our sake, he stayed in his right mind.

UNTAMED FAITH

You cannot meet the Creator of the universe and remain the same. If the God who is all-powerful, all-knowing, and all-present comes to dwell within your soul, you would expect at least some minor disruption. I think there's a problem when people talk about meeting God or knowing God and yet remain unchanged by God. When the Creator chooses to dwell within His creation, there is transformation. If Jesus has come to dwell within you, you are no longer suited for a normal life.

To have the Spirit of God dwelling within the heart of someone who chooses a domesticated faith is like having a tiger trapped within a cage. You are not intended to be a spiritual zoo where people can look at God in you from a safe distance. You are a jungle where the Spirit roams wild and free in your life. You are the recipient of the God who cannot be tamed and of a faith that must not be tamed. You are no longer a prisoner of time and space, but a citizen of the kingdom of God—a resident of the barbarian tribe. God is not a sedative that keeps you calm and under control by dulling your senses. He does quite the opposite. He awakens your spirit to be truly alive.

This past year my daughter, Mariah, has been my travel companion on the barbarian way. She absolutely revels in the identity of being a barbarian. She gets it—you are most fully alive when you are on an adventure with God. Mariah loves to live and lives to love. While I love adventure and seem always drawn to risk, all my life I've been an accident waiting to happen. Mariah inherited my DNA. Put us together, and some kind of medical personnel or a rescue team is usually involved.

Our family was in New Zealand visiting some of our closest friends, the Crawfords. On one of our expeditions we went ATVing in the wild and beautiful terrain of *Lord of the Rings*. Even though she was only eleven at the time, we gave Mariah her own wheels. I have to admit I was pretty nervous watching her drive trails that banked against steep drops and led through moving streams and up and down steep hills. But when we hit the mud track, things got really exciting. Racing full speed ahead while getting caked with mud is as much as a barbarian could possibly hope for. It was the barbarian version of a mud bath right up until she lost control, hit the accelerator instead of the brake, and crashed head-on into her mother's parked ATV. Next stop, emergency room—a vital locale for the barbarian. Everyone was fine.

It was a bit embarrassing since the day before we had an incident while Jet Skiing off the coast of Wellington. I had taken the Jet Ski out by myself for a few wild and wide-open runs just to make sure everything would be okay. Then I came back and got Mariah. We were having a blast. Wind in our faces, water breaking in every direction, moving freely at breakneck speed. It was exhilarating. It was nothing less than a worship experience. Then we ended up with a dead engine, and we were drifting helplessly into Cook Strait.

Here is what happened. A moment before, we were moving wide open toward the strait, and then all of a sudden I felt Mariah let go. Her arms had been tightly secured around my waist, and the moment she released, I heard her yell, "Stop!"

Knowing she was in danger, I immediately shut down the Jet Ski and turned to secure her. I shouted, "What's wrong?"

Mariah's tone made it clear she thought it was obvious: "I needed to get my hair out of my eyes."

I had flooded the engine for cosmetic reasons. I guess it was about an hour later when the Wellington Rescue Squad came out and saved us. Did I mention that the water was frigid? As you can imagine, while we were drifting, we had a lot of time to talk and reflect. Just a bit irritated, I tried to understand why it was so important to get her hair out of her eyes.

It was so simple—she couldn't see. And isn't that the whole point of choosing to live an adventure—to keep your eyes wide open and to soak in the beauty of the life all around you? Mariah was not about to live through the experience with her eyes closed. Eyes wide open is exactly how God created us to live our lives. And this is exactly what Jesus has come to ensure—that we are awakened to live life wide open as we move full speed ahead.

When you join the barbarian tribe, you begin to live your life with your eyes and your heart wide open. When the Spirit of God envelops your soul, your spirit comes alive, and everything changes for you. You are no longer the same. And to those who cannot see the invisible, to those who refuse to believe it exists, the path you choose, the life you live, may lead them to conclude that you are not simply different but insane. People who are fully alive look out of their minds to those who simply exist.

A SPIRIT TRIBE

When I was twelve years old, I had my first visit to a psychiatrist. I had a lot of brokenness to deal with and a lot of junk to overcome. And after more than two decades of walking with Christ, I'm happy to say that while Jesus can wonderfully make you healthy, He has no ambition to make you normal. The healthier you become, the freer you are to simply be yourself. The more your identity is rooted in God's value for you, the less you are controlled and limited by what others think of you. If only fools fall in love and people who are in love act like fools, then those who are changed by God's love really do become fools for Christ.

Reading the Scriptures, I find a history of people who were driven out of their minds by the living God. God would continually call them to believe things they could not see, become someone they were not, accomplish feats that were clearly beyond their abilities, and then hold them accountable for it. Certainly that would be maddening. Yet for all who accepted the barbarian call, the same thing happened—they became different aliens.

Peter put it like this: "You are a chosen people, a royal priesthood, a holy nation, a people belonging to God, that you may declare the praises of him who called you out of darkness into his wonderful light. Once you were not a people, but now you are the people of God; once you had not received mercy, but now you have received mercy" (1 Peter 2:9–10).

He went on to describe us as aliens and strangers in the world; all of us different, but a part of the same tribe; all of us walking in the same direction, but on a unique path; all of us becoming what we could not be without the One who created us. When barbarians travel together, they do not march in single file. There is no forced conformity. They are not required or expected to keep in step. They walk together as free individuals joined not by standardization, but by spirit.

MYSTICAL AND MIRACULOUS

Just a few months after becoming a follower of Jesus Christ, I found myself back at college, but on an entirely new mission. I didn't know a whole lot about Christianity, so I went to everything that looked as if it was associated with the faith. I went to Catholic Mass, to a Baptist church, to a charismatic fellowship, to an interdenominational Bible study, and I worked on a project with the Church of Christ. I pretty much covered the entire spectrum of the Christian faith. It was like a buffet—all you can eat for $2.49. You know the kind of college meal I'm talking about—high consumption with low quality. I didn't care how good it was; I just wanted all I could get.

In one of those groups I had come to know a young woman who led worship. I was just learning how to play the guitar so she lent me her guitar throughout the week. One day, to my surprise, Beth came to me and began sharing openly about her life before she met Christ. She explained that she used to live with a guy, and she had just talked to him and decided to go back to him. Her motivations to turn back to her old life were surely more complex than she explained, but all she told me was that she didn't feel God anymore. Her conclusion was that God simply didn't love her. Sometimes it's easier to believe in a love you can touch than a love that is real.

When she told me that a part of her previous life involved drug abuse, it all began to make more sense. God is not a drug, and He certainly does not create experiences and emotions that make us feel better but not become better. I have to tell you I was shocked. She looked like the perfect church girl.

I was still learning that Christians can look great on the outside and be an absolute mess on the inside.

When she unloaded all of that on me, I had no idea what to do. I was pretty new at the whole thing and certainly had not been trained as a counselor. When she told me she didn't believe God loved her, I just knew that was wrong. Looking back, I realize I should have simply pointed her to the Cross. After all, His sacrifice is proof of His love. I just didn't think of it then. I'm always smarter after the crisis and pretty stupid during.

So when Beth accused God of not loving her, I turned to her and assured her that if there was anything God could do to prove His love to her, He would do it. I know better than to say that now, but I didn't know any better then. For some bizarre reason she immediately responded by saying, "Well, then I want it to snow."

Just imagine being in my place in that moment. In a million years it never would have occurred to me that this would be her response. I can't make it snow. I guess I kind of meant God would do whatever He needed to through me or someone else. You know, something "doable." And by the way, as a guy, I think this is why it's so difficult to communicate with women. A guy would have asked for a convertible or an F "miraculously" changed to an A or a date with a cheerleader—something reasonable.

What she asked for totally confused me. What I said in response confused me even more. All of a sudden I heard a voice saying, "God is going to make it snow for you." You can imagine my surprise when I realized that voice was mine. I suppose I can appeal to being in shock. As soon as I heard myself say that, I added, "Within twenty-four hours." I meant to say it would take Him more than twenty-four hours. I got it backward and ended up giving God and myself a time limit.

She left, celebrating that God was going to make it snow for her because He loved her. I left, feeling traumatized because it wasn't very likely to happen.

I went back to my dorm, pulled down the shades, and shut off the lights, and I got down on my face before God. Have you ever earnestly, desperately cried out to God? I don't know why I said what I said, but I can tell you, in that moment I was absolutely convinced God spoke to me and in some way spoke through me. I wasn't trying to be presumptuous; I certainly wasn't trying to claim I could perform a miracle. It was like a mental hiccup; the loss of oxygen created a spontaneous response. But it was too late. It was after the fact. All I could do was to beg God to be involved.

Honestly I blame God for the encounter. I was pretty sure He had put me up to it. On that basis I asked Him to please come through. But I'm also a realist. There was a real possibility that it wasn't God, that it was all just me, and that God was up in heaven yelling, "What were you thinking?"

I obviously don't remember everything I prayed that day, but part of it went something like this: "God, I don't know why I said that. I actually thought You said it, but if it wasn't You, could You sort of adopt the idea and take this project on?" I was crying out to God, praying desperately. I was out of my mind, and I fell asleep in the midst of my exhaustion. Several hours went by before my roommate, Mark, came back and awakened me. Just for the record, I think those hours I was asleep count as intercession. It's all about intent.

To my surprise, the first words out of his mouth were, "Have you looked outside?"

The first thing that crossed my mind was that somehow he knew. I was entirely unaware that Beth felt free to tell anyone she saw that God was going to make it snow for her since He loved her. I didn't tell her to do that. It never occurred to me that she wouldn't keep my insanity a secret. I realize now that I was at a deficit since I had read only the gospel of John. If only I had read the gospel of Mark. In Mark, after Jesus performed a miracle on someone's behalf, He said, "Go and tell no one." Having that knowledge would have been really helpful. I could have reduced the level of potential humiliation and sounded spiritual at the same time.

I wasn't at all sure what was motivating Mark's question. Was he mocking me or trying to warn me that I'd better get to work if this thing was going to turn out well? With little conversation I simply got up and walked over to the window. I remember taking a deep breath just before I pulled open the shades. I don't know what I was expecting to see, but I saw snow everywhere. Evidently it had started snowing almost immediately after I began my soulful conversation with God.

Of course, this is where I'm supposed to tell you I knew the whole time that it would snow, never had any doubts, never worried. But I still don't know how it happened. I'm not trying to explain it, just trying to share this story with you as

I experienced it. I'll never forget the warm feeling I had while running across that snow and finding this young woman playing in the gift that God sent just for her. At least on that day God changed her mind. It was on the same day that God drove me out of mine. Later I would go to seminary and learn that God doesn't speak like this anymore. Essentially I was told that God exchanged the mystical and miraculous for doctrine and ritual. What the Spirit once did, programs have now replaced, and even the Scriptures became proof that God had stopped speaking.

But what was I to do? I had already experienced God in both the mystical and the miraculous. God had already turned me into a barbarian. You could put a suit on me, but underneath there would always be a savage. Once the primal fires have been ignited, fluorescent lights just won't do. I could have rationalized everything I experienced. The problem was that it wasn't an isolated event. Those who brought me to the faith did not take the time to civilize me. They brought me to the barbarian way and never tried to make me like them— only like Christ. They brought me into the presence of the living God and knew that His presence would both consume me and transform me.

CLOUDED THINKING

In the closing verses of Exodus that barbarian journey is described this way:

> The cloud covered the Tent of Meeting, and the glory
> of the LORD filled the tabernacle. Moses could not
> enter the Tent of Meeting because the cloud had set-
> tled upon it, and the glory of the LORD filled the tab-
> ernacle. In all the travels of the Israelites, whenever
> the cloud lifted from above the tabernacle, they
> would set out; but if the cloud did not lift, they did
> not set out—until the day it lifted. So the cloud of
> the LORD was over the tabernacle by day, and fire was
> in the cloud by night, in the sight of all the house of
> Israel during all their travels. (Exodus 40:34–38)

The civilized build shelters and invite God to stay with them;
barbarians move with God wherever He chooses to go. The
civilized Christian has a routine; the barbarian disciple has a
mission. The civilized believer knows the letter of the law; the
barbarian disciple lives the spirit of the law. The religiously

civilized love tradition; the barbarian spirit loves challenges. The civilized are satisfied with ritual; barbarians live and thrive in the mystical. For the civilized disciple, religion provides stability and certainty; for the barbarian, a life in God is one of risk and mystery.

And maybe even a little insanity. There's no way to escape that barbarians can appear out of their minds. No reasonable person would ever fully follow God everywhere He calls. God is simply unreasonable.

No matter how we try to spin the story, the Bible is filled with tribes of irrational people. When Noah built the ark, he did not live in a flood zone. When Elijah called fire down from heaven, he had never tried it before. Go ahead. Give it a shot. See if it works for you. I didn't think so. David should have left the giant alone. Hosea never should have married a prostitute. What was Moses thinking when he pointed his staff at the Red Sea—that it would move because he commanded it? And that's just to mention the more popular and highly admired followers of God.

Those people did not live normal lives. Their actions were ludicrous and irrational if you take God out of the formula. Given proper counseling, they would have known better than to do what they did. The vitality of their life in God moved them beyond the practicality of simply being reasonable. Their lives didn't make sense, their actions defied sensibility, because God drove them out of their senses. Anyone who ever risks listening to God and following His voice knows that to everyone who is deaf to His voice, your actions will seem as if you've gone crazy.

I used to serve on the Board of Intercultural Studies at Biola University, mostly because a friend of mine asked me if I would. But after a while I wondered why I said yes. I almost never went. I hate meetings. I would much rather be outdoors than in a boardroom. Usually I asked, "Do you want me in the morning, afternoon, or evening?" I couldn't get myself to commit to the whole day.

One afternoon I happened to be there when the counseling department enthusiastically presented a plan for serving missionary personnel around the world. They were going to provide access to counseling and mental health to all those working overseas. Even while I was listening, I knew I should remain silent. I kept telling myself to keep my mouth shut: *Don't say anything; don't cause any problems; don't embarrass yourself.* But I just couldn't help myself.

Before I knew it I was blurting out, "Don't do it. Please don't do it."

They all looked at me with the strangest expressions of confusion.

Well, it was too late for me to hide in obscurity, so I knew I needed to explain. I went on, "Don't go around the world and make our missionaries mentally healthy. You'll ruin everything. You'll totally mess up the cause. I mean you have, let's say, a husband and a wife from Kentucky and they have four kids and they believe God has called them to an obscure city in Central Asia. Suddenly they find themselves in the middle of two million people who don't speak a word of English, and they don't speak a word of Mandarin or Cantonese or any form of tribal dialect. And each morning they wake up excited and confident that somehow they're going to bring that entire city to faith in Jesus Christ. You go and make them normal, and they'll be on a plane back home the next day."

The board member making the presentation graciously responded, "Erwin clearly has a different view of professional counseling than we do."

These people have got to be crazy to do what they're

doing and insane to believe that it's possible, don't they? They are not insane, but they are crazy. One day they just got up and took the barbarian way out of civilization.

If you are a follower of Christ and you have allowed yourself to be domesticated, you have lost the power of who you are and who God intends for you to be. You were not created to be normal. God's desire for you is not compliance and conformity. You have been baptized by Spirit and fire. Asleep within you is a barbarian, a savage to all who love the prim and proper. You must go to the primal place and enter the presence of the Most High God, for there you will be changed by His presence. Let Him unleash the untamed faith within you.

GOD-TAUGHT

At pentecost God unleashed His Spirit upon all who would declare Jesus their hope. In that moment a new tribe was born—a Spirit tribe. To all who would believe in His Son, the Lord God declares, "I will be their God, and they will be My people." This tribe would bear the evidence of His Spirit. They would be God-taught, God-moved, and God-inspired.

Our spiritual legacy is that we belong to this barbarian tribe. From the first human to the present, the history of God is one of conversation and transformation. The Scriptures are filled with stories of women and men who heard God speak and acted as if hearing Him were normal. Hearing God is not only to be normal, but also to be an essential proof of belonging to God. To be taught by God is one of the primal evidences that you have entered the new covenant ushered in by Jesus. In Jeremiah 31:33–34, the Lord declares:

> "This is the covenant I will make with
>> the house of Israel
>> after that time," declares the LORD.
> "I will put my law in their minds
>> and write it on their hearts.
> I will be their God,
>> and they will be my people.
> No longer will a man teach his neighbor,
>> or a man his brother, saying, 'Know the LORD,'
>> because they will all know me,
>> from the least of them to the greatest."

To study the Bible is important, but it is not a primal evidence that you belong to God. Anyone can study the Bible, but only those who know Him can hear His voice and are taught by Him. Although the barbarian may not be formally trained, she is always God-taught. Jesus expected that those who were His followers would hear His voice, know His voice, and follow only His voice, even as He calls us out by name and leads us on the barbarian way.

HEARING VOICES

My son, Aaron, was probably five or six when he began asking me about the voice of God. He would often hear me talk about having conversations with God (most of us call this prayer), and it piqued his curiosity. On top of that, week by week he heard me teach and share mystical and miraculous experiences with God. I should have been prepared for the question, but it actually caught me off guard. When he asked me, "What does God's voice sound like?" I really didn't know how to answer. I guess when I think about it, God's voice sounds a lot like my voice. After all, the Spirit speaks to us through the conscience as well as through the Scriptures. Even when I'm reading the Scriptures, the voice I'm hearing is mine reading the text. In my experience the voice of God is an intimate experience, but not an audible one. Or at least it's not a voice coming from the outside in, but a voice coming from deep within.

I can't quite remember what I told him. Keep in mind, he was only five or six. I think my response was something like, "That's a great question. Now go watch cartoons."

A few years later, after many other similar inquiries, Aaron went off to his first junior high camp in Big Bear, about two hours from Los Angeles. Somewhere in the middle of the week, one of the other pastors at Mosaic, whose daughter was also at the camp, decided to go up with me so we could see our kids.

I expected to find Aaron having a great time, growing in the Lord, and making new friends. Instead, he had gotten himself into deep trouble. Evidently on their first lunch break he was involved in a fight. But it wasn't really a fight; it was sort of a "prefight." You know, the stuff guys do before the fight because they don't really want to fight.

Anyway, some kid said something, and Aaron said something back. The tension heightened, the smack deepened, and the next thing you know, Aaron's lunging at him and his friends are holding him back. By the time I got there two days had passed, and Aaron refused to ask for forgiveness. And if acting on his hostility wasn't bad enough, he had to go off and be the classic son of a preacher. In typical male form, he had to describe what he was going to do to his antagonist before he proceeded to do it. In short, he yelled out, "I'm going to beat the crap out of you." (In case you're wondering, *crap* is not an acceptable descriptive term used in our home.) I went to celebrate my son's spiritual pilgrimage, and I found myself in the middle of an all-out war.

I knew the Lord was working already because when Aaron tried to assault the other kid, his friends held him back. The other kid was huge and probably would have killed Aaron. We already had something to be grateful for.

When I confronted Aaron and asked him if the story I was given was accurate, he said, "Absolutely." He didn't deny anything. He also wasn't sorry for anything. I told him he needed to ask for forgiveness, and he told me that wasn't going to happen. He wasn't sorry, he would do it again, and upon reflection, he was sorry for only one thing—he didn't get at least one good punch in before they brought him down.

Trying to understand what in the world could have made Aaron so angry, I asked him to tell me what motivated him to attack the kid. Aaron said, "Dad, I don't care what you say. He said something about Mom. Anyone who says something about my mom is going to have to deal with me."

You can imagine my response: "He said something about your mom? What did he say about your mom?" I have to admit, I was with him.

Anyway, I still insisted that he needed to make things right. He said he would not, and in fact, he insisted on being allowed to leave the camp. He reminded me that I had committed to him that he would never have to pretend or play the Christian game. I told him if that's what he wanted to do, he could leave. I also told him I felt it was a mistake. He insisted and asked me if I would help him pack. I said no, I wouldn't stop him from leaving, but I wouldn't help him leave either. So for the next hour he put together his stuff, dragged it up the hill, and pushed it into the car.

Just as we were about to leave, I asked him to sit with me and talk one last time before we drove away. We sat on two large rocks in the middle of the woods. I asked him a simple question: "Aaron, is there any voice inside you telling you what you should do?"

He paused and then responded, "Yes."

"What's the voice telling you?"

"That I should stay and work it out."

I asked him, "Can you identify that voice?"

He immediately said, "Yes. It's God."

It was the moment I had waited for. I didn't expect it to come under those circumstances. Nevertheless, it was there. I turned to Aaron and said, "Aaron, do you realize what just happened? You just heard the voice of the living God. He spoke to you from within your soul. Forget everything else that just happened. God has spoken to you, and you were able to recognize Him."

I'll never forget his response: "Well, I'm still not doing what He said."

I explained to him that was his choice, but this is what would happen. If he rejected the voice of God and chose to disobey His guidance, his heart would become hardened, and his ears would become dull. And if he continued on this path, there would be a day when he would never again hear the voice of God. There would come a day when he would deny that God even speaks or has ever spoken to him. But if he treasured God's voice and responded to Him with obedience, then his heart would be softened, and his ears would always be able to hear the whisper of God into his soul.

Aaron chose to stay, I'm grateful to say. If he had chosen differently, he would have begun the path toward domestication. Perhaps he never would have rejected the faith overtly. He might have even chosen to be a faithful attender at a church and been by everyone else's estimation a good man, but he would no longer be a barbarian.

ENCOUNTERED

Years later when Aaron was about fourteen, I saw this so clearly. We were driving in the car together and had one of those gut-wrenching heart-to-heart talks. "Dad, I think that if I had not been raised in a Christian home, I would not be a Christian," he said.

You can imagine the rush of emotions going through me. It took all the restraint I had to not panic and stay calm. "Why do you think that?" I asked as if his statement had no emotional effect on me.

Aaron continued, "I have way too many doubts and questions."

"Oh," I said, sounding as relieved as I could. "I have those too. So what are you going to do?"

I'll never forget Aaron's answer. It was one of the clearest confirmations that my son was not an unwilling member of a religion, that he, too, was a true barbarian. "Well, I've met God. So what are you supposed to do?"

I affirmed, "That's a dilemma, isn't it?"

So many of us have put our hope in teaching our children about God rather than guiding them into an experience with God. We essentially civilize our children rather than guide them to the barbarian way. I am concerned that there are many who have grown up in church and have been effectively Christianized but have never genuinely met Christ. In the days of Jonathan Edwards, he faced the same dilemma when the congregation of his time had a Halfway Covenant. The children of members were essentially Christians who had never met Christ. His classic message, "Sinners in the Hands of an Angry God," was directed not to the unchurched, but to the church. Our goal must not be to populate the Christian religion but to bring people into a genuine relationship with God. We must make a clear distinction between the religion of Christianity and the revolution that Jesus began two thousand years ago.

GOD-MOVED

A second primal evidence of the barbarian spirit is unleashed when you enter into covenant with God. Not only are you God-taught as a disciple of the living God, but you are also God-moved. God informed us that He has a strategy for reestablishing His reputation among the nations:

> Say to the house of Israel, "This is what the Sovereign LORD says: It is not for your sake, O house of Israel, that I am going to do these things, but for the sake of my holy name, which you have profaned among the nations where you have gone. I will show the holiness of my great name, which has been profaned among

the nations, the name you have profaned among them. Then the nations will know that I am the LORD, declares the Sovereign LORD, *when I show myself holy through you* before their eyes." (Ezekiel 36:22–23, italics added)

God made an emphatic declaration that He will prove He is God and He is holy not through His action but through the actions of His people. A civilized faith relates to right and wrong as a moral obligation. A barbarian faith loves good and hates evil. There is no obligation fueling the actions of His people. They are passionate about the very things that are on the heart of God. Their motivation is not external, but intrinsic. They are moved from the inside out. Speaking again of this new covenant, God described what this primal transformation will look like:

I will give you a new heart and put a new spirit in you; I will remove from you your heart of stone and give you a heart of flesh. And *I will put my Spirit in you and move you to follow* my decrees and be careful to keep my laws. You will live in the land I gave your

forefathers; you will be my people, and I will be your
God. (Ezekiel 36:26–28, italics added)

From the moment we become citizens of the kingdom of
God, we become aliens and strangers in a world that chooses
to live absent of God. From the first step taken to follow Jesus,
we are out of step with the rest of the world. Once your life is
in sync with the story of God, you become out of sync with
any story that attempts to ignore or eliminate God. You are a
stranger to them, an alien among them, a nomadic wanderer
who, while refusing to be rooted in this life, seems to somehow enjoy this life most.

Probably motivated by movies such as *Men in Black*,
Aaron once asked me if there really were aliens among us. I
told him that of course there were, and that we had to reg-
ister with the government to gain peaceful admission. A bit
unnerved, he asked me if I was implying that I was an alien. I
told him that while I had chosen to keep this confidential in
the past, it was a good time to let him know the truth: I was
an alien in this land. He said, "Prove it."

I pulled out my green card that had my picture and the
declaration "Resident Alien." I tried to calm him down by

assuring him that he was still half human. It didn't seem to help. Okay, so I'm only from El Salvador. Not quite as glamorous as being Vulcan or Romulan, but an alien nonetheless. It's ironic that now our entire family is legitimately alien. Our citizenship is in eternity; history is our temporary residence. You are no different. Every one of us who hears the barbarian call of Christ and chooses to follow will become a foreigner and perhaps even an outcast in the time and place in which we live.

John the Baptist heard the voice of God and became an outcast among those to whom God was silent. His life was short, and if his death lacked anything, it was dignity; yet he was considered great in the sight of God. First pointing to him, Jesus then pointed to us. He promised that the least in the kingdom of heaven would be greater than even John. Jesus was pronouncing the coming of a tribe. Where there was one, there would soon be millions.

All who belong to the barbarian tribe are like Moses, who stepped toward the fire and heard the voice of God. For them the whole earth is holy ground. They do not separate between sacred and secular or real life and spiritual life. All of life is sacred; every action is spiritual. God is everywhere for them and in all things at all times.

WATER GRAVE

One Sunday morning a young woman named Nicole and her friends introduced me to Dathan. Dathan is one of those guys who stands out in the crowd—built like a rock, big smile, charismatic personality. Dathan lives in Los Angeles and is pursuing a career as an actor. He's also in the process of preparing for tryouts, hoping to make it as a defensive back in the NFL. Having grown up in Philly, he had chosen the path of hard-core crime and violence, so it was strange that my first conversation with him was about fear.

He had just become a follower of Jesus Christ, and Nicole had asked him if he was ready to be baptized. Her question evoked an unexpected response. He was terrified. So they brought him to me so that I could talk him through it. After brief introductions, I asked him to tell me what the problem was. He explained that he was afraid of water. The baptism was planned for Dockweiler Beach, and he just didn't feel he could go through with it.

I asked him if he was just afraid of the ocean or if there was more to it. He went on to explain that he was terrified of sharks. Later I learned that when he was about eleven years old, he was in the water and saw one of his friends being attacked. He was an eyewitness to a horrific and tragic event. It had been many years, but the memories of that event still haunted him.

I told him that there were other options. We could baptize him in a pool or even a Jacuzzi. That seemed to alleviate his concern a bit, and he began to relax. Then I added, "But that would sort of be the easy way out. You don't look like the kind of guy who takes the easy way out of anything." I went on, "What do you think is the likelihood you would get eaten by a shark the day you're baptized? I mean, the percentages have to be really low—like one in a million or maybe one in a thousand. Anyway, it's really unlikely that you would be attacked by a shark if you chose to be baptized in the ocean."

He nodded in agreement, but my comments clearly didn't help.

"Well, think of it like this," I said. "The likelihood is so low that you would get attacked by a shark, you would know it was God's will for your life if a shark did attack you." I don't know why, but the thought wasn't all that comforting to him. Then I added, "But if you live, if perchance no shark kills you and you survive the experience, then you will know without a shadow of a doubt that God has kept you alive, that He has a purpose for you to fulfill." I closed our conversation by concluding, "I think the pool or Jacuzzi would be okay for someone else, but I think for you it's going to have to be the ocean."

I left him with a decision to make. Would he hear the barbarian call, or would he immediately choose to be domesticated?

It wasn't long before Dathan informed me that he was headed to the beach. He had an appointment with destiny. To facilitate his experience, I asked some of my friends to take him to a shark reserve so he could spend some time with his friends. On the day of his baptism, the waves were strong and the waters rough. One man walked on each side of him as he worked his way out deeper into the ocean. A wave hit him head-on and knocked the other two men into the water, but Dathan, determined not to go under until he had to, grabbed both and willed them back up.

After he was immersed in the ocean and worked his way to the beach, he threw himself into the sand and wept. I asked him later what overwhelmed him. He said it wasn't fear; it was the knowledge that God had a purpose for his life.

Now you might be thinking this is a bit of overkill or even emotionally abusive, but if I've learned anything over the years, it's that it is a grave error to try to domesticate a barbarian. We live in a world of wandering barbarians who do not know God. They have no interest in civilized religion and no time for the games of the proper and refined. Dathan had acted on the worst of his passions, and nothing but a new passion would set him free. Dathan needed to understand that it was a life-and-death decision.

It shouldn't surprise us that Paul described baptism as a water grave. He chose this imagery to describe this sacred passage: "Don't you know that all of us who were baptized into Christ Jesus were baptized into his death? We were therefore buried with him through baptism into death in order that, just as Christ was raised from the dead through the glory of the Father, we too may live a new life" (Romams 6:3–4).

Only a few months after his baptism, Dathan landed a part in a movie pulling together a potential cast of Ed Norton, Nicolas Cage, and Taye Diggs. His, of course, was a smaller part, but in the midst of it he had to make a big decision. He was offered a scene that would be standard in the industry but was now beneath his standards. It would have been easy for Dathan to justify the fact that it's just the way of the civilized, but he chose to follow his barbarian call. He turned down a scene that could have helped establish his career and chose instead to establish his character. His decision wasn't about legalism; he was moved from the inside out to do what would bring God pleasure and honor His name. And like Dathan, all of us, if we are to follow Jesus with the passion He desires and deserves, must face the sharks and never submit to them.

We're all called to pass through the water grave. Yes, the way into the tribe of God is barbaric. You are joined with the death of Christ, buried with Him, and raised to live again. The barbarian has tasted death, has faced death, has conquered death. What do you fear when you have already died and you walked away? Your greatest fears are behind you, and you now go where only those once dead, yet alive, can go. It is here where the third primal expression of the barbarian spirit is born in every follower of Christ. The barbarian way is a path where we are God-taught and God-moved, but we are also God-inspired.

GOD-INSPIRED

The prophet Joel described the catalytic effect of the barbarian spirit ignited by the new covenant:

> I will pour out my Spirit on all people.
> Your sons and daughters will prophesy,
>> your old men will dream dreams,
>> your young men will see visions.
> Even on my servants, both men and women,
>> I will pour out my Spirit in those days.
> (Joel 2:28–29)

God's ultimate end for our transformation is to unleash the untamed faith within. When His Spirit is poured into our lives, we are inspired to an extraordinary level of living. Barbarians never exist simply to survive. Barbarians never just get through the day. Barbarians wake to live and live life fully awake. To be filled with the Spirit of God is to be filled with dreams and visions that are too compelling to ignore. Live or die, succeed or fail, barbarians must pursue and attempt such dreams and visions. The barbarian spirit dreams great dreams and finds the courage to live them.

The barbarian call confronts us with all we love and all we fear. We resist love to avoid pain and squelch our dreams out of fear of failure. For the Spirit of God to unleash dreams and visions within our souls, we must become free to risk and to fail. Every dream born of God is fueled by love. Every conversation to be had with God challenges the boundaries of our imagination. When we turn to God, His love transforms us and ignites a new passion within us. All that we have loved is consumed by the passions of a new heart. We discover the power and force of love in its purest form. At the same time, when we turn our hearts toward God, all of our fears are consumed by one fear. We are called to fear only God. There is an important reason for this. What we fear is what we're subject to; our fears define our master. Where there is no fear, there is no control.

When we fear God and God only, we are no longer bound by all of the other fears that would hold us captive. The fear of death, the fear of failure, the fear of rejection, the fear of insignificance—all of the fears that know us by name and haunt us in the dark of the night become powerless when we know the fear of the Lord. And if this is not enough, we discover that perfect love casts out all fear. Not even God will hold us or control us by fear. When we fear Him, we in essence begin to live a life where we are fearless.

The freedom to love and the freedom from fear make the barbarian an entirely different species within the whole of humanity. This may be the most extraordinary mark of the Spirit of God within the heart of humanity: the freedom to live out dreams greater than ourselves. Yet if we were honest with ourselves, the church would be the last place most people would go to have their dreams nurtured, developed, and unleashed.

FESTIVAL OF LIFE

One of the great joys I've been privileged to experience as a result of writing *Chasing Daylight* has been receiving the stories of people from all over the world who have chosen to redirect their lives to pursue the dreams that had remained latent within them. As lead pastor of Mosaic, I regard this as an essential measure of spiritual health and vitality. When the church becomes an institution, people are nothing more than volunteers to be recruited. When the church is a movement, our stewardship becomes the unleashing of our God-given gifts, talents, and passions. My goal is not to cast a vision that everyone buys into, but to create a visional community where everyone who enters in begins to have wild and God-sized dreams and visions. There is a price to pay, of course, when you choose this particular path; you end up with an unruly barbarian tribe. They keep getting called by God to do things you didn't expect or really didn't want them to do.

From our community in Los Angeles we have social workers in New Delhi; artists in Istanbul; an aspiring chef in Paris; a dancer, a film editor, a soon-to-be doctor, and a fashion designer in New York; businesspeople in China; a psychologist and educator in Lithuania; an environmental engineer in Morocco; and the list goes on and on and on. I cannot overemphasize how difficult these people are to replace. Yet as much complexity as this brings and as much instability as this creates, it pales in comparison to watching lives being wasted on careers and occupations that were taken on as a result of obligation or lack of courage to pursue the dreams that were waiting to be realized.

While modern man keeps hoping we will evolve into something that will be godlike, the barbarian way unveils that our best future is found in our primal beginnings. Evolution is not the key to humanity's freedom; transformation is. There is a metamorphosis waiting to happen within every one of us. A part of this metamorphosis is discovering your divine destiny and knowing for the first time who you were created to become. When the Spirit of God comes to live within you, you strangely become aware of your inadequacy and your extraordinary potential. When you choose the path of a civilized religion, any change that is worth noting is at best incremental. It is only when you choose the barbarian way that the result is revolutionary.

Recently I heard an old Celtic proverb that says you should never give a sword to a man who can't dance. This couldn't be more true than on the barbarian way. Every mystic warrior finds his strength from his inner joy. This is what Nehemiah declared as he called God's people to rise up and face their impending challenge: "Go and enjoy choice food and sweet drinks, and send some to those who have nothing prepared. This day is sacred to our Lord. Do not grieve, for the joy of the LORD is your strength" (Nehemiah 8:10).

You have now joined a tribe of dreamers and visionaries,

and this is no small part of why you are passionate to bring others into this community of faith, hope, and love. You have found through the liberation of your soul that each barbarian walks a path that unleashes raw and untamed faith.

4

THE
BARBARIAN
REVOLT

From the days of John the Baptist until now, the kingdom of heaven has been forcefully advancing, and forceful men lay hold of it. (Matthew 11:12)

Not long ago Aaron asked me, "Dad, would you purposefully put us in danger?"

"Yes," I answered, "of course."

Without blinking an eye his response was simply, "That's what I thought. I was just making sure." I could tell he was tying together all the pieces of his more recent travels. In retrospect, he could see more clearly the reality of the danger and volatility of which he had been in the midst.

I wonder how many of us have actually had this conversation with God: "Abba, Father, Dad, would You purposefully put me in danger?" I think a lot of us haven't asked God that question because we went ahead and answered it for Him. Of course He wouldn't do that. We're His children. We're family. He wouldn't purposefully endanger us, not even to accomplish a higher or nobler purpose. Or would He? Maybe you should stop and ask Him. His answer might surprise you. It certainly surprised John the Baptist.

There is a barbarian revolt taking place, and its command center is the kingdom of God. Everywhere the kingdom of God advances, there is a violent engagement against a dark kingdom. To be born of God is to be made a citizen in the kingdom of God, and the kingdom of God is at war. Do not confuse this kingdom with Paradise. Salvation is not reentry into a Paradise Lost; it is enlistment in the mission of God.

Jesus is telling us in no uncertain terms that there is a battle raging. This is perhaps the most important reason why we must choose the barbarian way and resist any temptation to become civilized. Domesticated Christians are far too willing to abdicate the battle for the soul of the world. Civility focuses our energy on all the wrong places. We spend our lives emphasizing our personal development and spiritual well-being. We build churches that become nothing more than hiding places for the faithful while pretending that our actions are for the good of the world. Or we choose political and secular vehicles to try to advance our cultural values, strangely attempting to make unbelieving people act like civilized believers.

In contrast Jesus calls us to a different way. He tells us this is a battle of kingdoms. He insists that if we are His followers, we must not live in a world defined only by the material. We cannot limit our sights to what is flesh and blood. We should know better than that. To see from a kingdom perspective is to know that there is a conflict of invisible kingdoms and that people's lives are forever changed by what happens in the unseen. We are called to be warriors of light in dark places. We are mystical warriors who use weapons not of this world.

A DIVINE INSURRECTION

For centuries the nations that have considered themselves civilized have chosen weapons that wield pain and destruction on the weak and innocent. The Romans, borrowing the phrase from the Greeks, described as *barbarians* all who were not of Rome. And certainly the Romans exemplify the great virtues of civilization. From violence to decadence, they could justify the most cruel and base actions against all who were not a part of them since the "others" were beneath them.

It's appropriate that the first Christians were barbarians to Rome. History tells us there came a day when the same barbarians turned Rome upside down. Tragically it wasn't long before Rome seduced and civilized the early church. The church did, in fact, become Roman. The church became civilized. And soon the same violence and decadence defined the Christian faith rather than opposed it. We put on robes, built cathedrals, accumulated wealth and power, then lost our barbarian way.

We find Judaism in the same tragic condition during the days of Jesus. Really it's an incredibly strange scenario to watch. Given that Jesus Himself is the God of Israel, it should strike us as extraordinary that He was not welcome there. But then again, Jesus didn't like it there. One of Jesus' most violent moments took place in the temple. He became disgusted by what He saw. He was so incensed by how Judaism had become a religious retail business that He began to destroy all of the sellers' merchandise.

It's important to point out that Jesus was not against business. His anger wasn't a response to people selling something of value or providing a meaningful service. His anger was evoked because the sellers of goods had made access to God a business. They had made forgiveness something you could purchase. They had made the guilt and shame of others the marketplace for their profit. They had made the house of God into a den of robbers and thieves. They had become so good at religion that they had no need for God. They were so full of themselves that they had no room for God. When it came down to it, they loved their civilized religion far more than they longed to know the God who created them. They treasured the civilization built around their religion and despised the primal faith from which it was born. They would rather have the temple than the Presence.

So Jesus let them have it, which begs the question: What good is a house of God if God no longer chooses to live there? Speaking of His own body, Jesus challenged them to destroy the temple, and God would raise it up after three days. They thought He meant the work of art built by the hands of men. They could not for a moment imagine that God would choose so barbaric a container as flesh and blood. It shouldn't surprise us that soon after they destroyed the Temple of God, God destroyed their temple.

There may be no clearer place where we see the division between the civilized and the barbarian. We discover the painful reality that even God's people, when we become civilized, are more than willing to crucify God. When we choose a civilized faith, God becomes, at the very least, an irritant and, at worst, an enemy to our faith. We find in Jesus that the hostility of God turns toward empty religion and the mercy of God turns toward the outcast and sinner. The way that Jesus called the masses to choose was far too barbaric for those who held the positions of religious leadership. The claim that He must become the sacrificial Lamb who would take away the sins of the world was an insult to their sense of piety and self-righteousness.

But maybe the most insulting thing that Jesus said or did was to become the friend of sinners. He focused His ministry on women and men who were despised by those in spiritual authority. The path God chose for Himself was far too common for their sensibility. They couldn't imagine that God would choose that kind of life for Himself. God would be above such things. God was far too civilized to choose such barbarism.

Luke described this conflict between Jesus and the religious leaders of His time as he followed the conversion of Levi:

> After this, Jesus went out and saw a tax collector by the name of Levi sitting at his tax booth. "Follow me," Jesus said to him, and Levi got up, left everything and followed him. Then Levi held a great banquet for Jesus at his house, and a large crowd of tax collectors and others were eating with them. But the Pharisees and the teachers of the law who belonged to their sect complained to his disciples, "Why do you eat and drink with tax collectors and 'sinners'?" Jesus answered them, "It is not the healthy who need a doctor, but the sick. I have not come to call the righteous, but sinners to repentance." (Luke 5:27–32)

LOVE UNTAMED

Two thousand years ago God started a revolt against the religion He started. So don't ever put it past God to cause a groundswell movement against churches and Christian institutions that bear His name. If He was willing to turn Judaism upside down, don't think for a moment our institutions are safe from a divine revolt. I am convinced that even now there are multitudes of followers of Jesus Christ who are sick and tired of the church playing games and playing down the call of God. My travels only confirm that the murmurings of revolution are everywhere. I am convinced that there is an uprising in the works and that no one less than God is behind it.

Anyone who can picture Jesus as the great Advocate of tradition is doing some serious doctoring of biblical history. Jesus was anything but the poster child for status quo. With a band of brothers and a small community of others, Jesus instigated an uprising that He expected to reach the very ends of the earth. You must never forget that it was only to a handful of individuals that Jesus entrusted an outcome that would make disciples of all the nations of the earth. The uprising was to transcend culture, ethnicity, race, religion, status—every and any divide established by men.

The driving purpose of this barbarian revolt is to liberate every person who longs to find freedom in God. Like barbarians destroying civilization, they are to remove every nonessential obstacle between God and man. Let no one remain captive to the nefarious schemes of religionists who attempt to hold God for ransom. Let nothing prevent you or hinder you from providing mercy and forgiveness to those living under the burden of guilt and shame. Who could have guessed that a message of love could incite so much hostility?

Barbarians are entrusted with the gospel—not a message of judgment and condemnation, but good news from God to humanity. Yet the opposition and persecution came with a force that could not be expected or even imagined. Ironically Jesus was crucified not in spite of His love, but because of it. Somehow love incites both love and hate with equal force. The mission of Christ would be so easy to embrace and carry out if love always resulted in love, but it does not. It seems the world insists that love be proved. So then those who claim love are required to endure hate's most brutal tests.

Wherever the love of Christ would be spread by His disciples, they encountered rejection, persecution, suffering, and even death.

Anyone who chooses the barbarian way will learn quickly that love and sacrifice cannot be separated. This is perhaps why so many of us who know love fear love. We know that love is not the absence of pain. If anything, love is the promise of pain. No one has loved more deeply than God. Has anyone ever been more betrayed? God would not know suffering if He did not know love. But because He is Love, He chose to suffer on our behalf. Without love there is no glory in suffering.

The suffering of Christ glorifies God because it elevates love. Compelled by love, God would go where He knew suffering was certain. Love always moves to sacrifice, which is exactly where He calls us to go. We shouldn't be surprised, then, that to follow Christ is to abandon the luxury of safety and security. If we are to be like Him, we must always risk for love. We are invited to follow Him with reckless abandon. The call of God is more than a leap of faith; it is a life of faith. Even when it seems beyond our abilities, we should not be surprised when God tells us to jump.

JUMP SCHOOL

For several years we rented a two-story house in Los Angeles. Both my kids had spent a good part of their childhood enjoying that home. A unique feature of the house was that a small window from the second-story bathroom opened a path to the roof. I always figured there would be a day when one of my kids would climb up on the sink and work his or her way out on the ledge. It just seemed to be one of those things that I or my brother, Alex, would have done when we were kids.

Early one evening Kim and I were in the front yard when all of a sudden, we heard a little voice calling for us from the roof. As soon as Kim saw him, her nurturing instinct kicked in, and she started commanding him to get back inside. I have to admit I was kind of proud of him right then, but what he did next totally surprised me.

Looking past his mom, he asked me if he could jump. When Aaron shouted, "Dad, can I jump?" Kim answered on my behalf, "No, you can't jump. Get back inside."

As if he hadn't heard anything at all, he asked me again, "Dad, can I jump?"

Now I know what I was supposed to do. A dad is never

supposed to override the mom (I'm working on it). I'm just telling you what really happened. After all, he did ask me. I answered, "Yeah, go ahead."

He said, "Really?"

I said, "Yeah, sure. Go ahead and jump."

Kim looked at me as if I was out of my mind and asked, "What do you think you're doing?"

In a sort of explanation I asked Aaron, "Aaron, are you going to jump sometime?"

He said, "Yeah, I think so."

I said, "Okay. I'd rather have you jump now so if you jump and break your legs, we can take you to the hospital." It made perfect sense to me.

He responded, "Dad, do you think I'll make it?"

I said, "Oh, yeah, you'll make it." If I knew one thing for certain, it was that he would reach the ground. I just wasn't sure in what condition.

He said, "Okay. I'm going to jump."

I had one suggestion before he took off. I said, "Hey, buddy, try to clear the concrete and land on the grass. It's softer."

He thought that was a good idea, stepped as far back as

he could on the roof, and began running to jump. Just before his first step he yelled, "Dad, catch me," and I said, "I'll try."

And he jumped.

I almost caught him. It was so close. He just slipped right through my hands. I think I did slow his fall a little bit. In either case, he's recovered well since then. I'm just kidding. He was fine. (Don't try this at home.)

WILDFIRE

I know it's very unlikely that you will ever invite me to speak at a parenting conference, but hang with me for a moment. From the parenting end, I've seen far too many kids raised in Christian homes who are indifferent to Christ and often carry a great disdain for the church. Sometimes it's the result of blatant hypocrisy, but other times it's the result of nothing less than sheer monotony and boredom. We raise our children in the cocoon of a domesticated faith and wonder why they run as far as they can to find adventure.

A long time ago I decided I would never let that happen to my children. I'm a first-generation Christian, but over the years I have seen the dangers that come with being the children of the second generation and beyond. First-generation believers, even when they are barbarians, often make the mistake of raising their children to be civilized.

Paul addressed that point in a letter to Timothy:

> I have been reminded of your sincere faith, which first lived in your grandmother Lois and in your mother Eunice and, I am persuaded, now lives in you also. For this reason I remind you to fan into flame the gift of God, which is in you through the laying on of my hands. For God did not give us a spirit of timidity, but a spirit of power, of love and of self-discipline. So do not be ashamed to testify about our Lord, or ashamed of me his prisoner. But join with me in suffering for the gospel, by the power of God, who has saved us and called us to a holy life—not because of anything we have done but because of his own purpose and grace. (2 Timothy 1:5–9)

Several times Paul encouraged Timothy to be identified with Christ and to not be ashamed of doing that. Connected to his encouragement, he called Timothy to not shrink back because of the suffering that he might face. If you read his letter carefully, it is the pleading of a barbarian who is losing his son in the faith to the way of the civilized. Paul called Timothy to reignite the fire that lay dormant within him. Paul was persuaded that Timothy had a genuine faith, but he was also equally convinced that the life Timothy was living did not reflect one who was alive in the Spirit. Timothy's problem wasn't blatant sin, but latent faith. Paul was calling Timothy to choose the barbarian way out of civilization.

Just yesterday a husband and wife told me that they raised their first son to be a gentleman, and now as a man he does not walk with Christ. They went on to say, "We have a second son, and we're going to raise him as a barbarian." They understood firsthand the painful difference between a civilized Christian and the barbarian way of Jesus.

How many stories do we need of children who grow up in church being forced to act like Christians rather than being won to the heart of God? Both are an effort to shape the character of our children. The first is an external force; the latter an internal force. The civilized Christian does what is right out of fear; the barbarian does what is right out of love. The

Christian civilization is held together by rules and rituals; the barbarian revolt is fueled by the passion of God and guided by the mission of God. If our children are going to walk away from Christ, we need to raise them in such a way that they understand that to walk away from Jesus is to walk away from a life of faith, risk, and adventure and to choose a life that is boring, mundane, and ordinary.

For Aaron, the jump was fraught with danger. From my vantage point, I could see, though the jump was terrifying, he would find himself triumphant. It was important that he jumped and perhaps even more important that he knew me as the kind of father who would always call him to greater endeavors rather than send him back to the safe place.

STAND ALONE

I think God is like that. For too long we've been telling followers of Jesus Christ to climb back through the window. Our message is that "God wants to keep you safe." We can't even see the importance of growing the courage to jump. But what if our house was on fire? What if Aaron's only memory was my telling him that he couldn't do it? What if I had, in that moment, nurtured fear and apprehension? Would he become the kind of person who would die out of fear of trying? What if the courage to jump or the lack of it would be the difference in saving someone else's life?

It may seem counterintuitive, but the more civilized we seem to become, the more detached from the pain of others we end up finding ourselves. The most civilized churches have really no practical concern for people outside their congregations. The brokenness of a lost and unbelieving world is not enough to inspire the painful changes necessary to make the church relevant to the world in which we live.

One of the tragedies of a civilized society is that no one wants to get involved. What becomes appropriate is to mind our own business. When we join a community that lacks a passionate heart for the world, we soon find ourselves acquiescing to apathy. It is a painful tragedy to see a brand-new follower of Christ alive with a barbarian spirit soon conformed to the status quo.

History again and again reveals to us that we are less likely to do good when we perceive ourselves a part of a larger crowd than if we make the choice standing alone. When we are in a crowd, we are more prone toward acts of evil or at least compliance to evil. For some reason the civilized can rationalize apathy and feel themselves absolved from personal responsibility. Good needs to be done, but someone else will take care of it.

The barbarian revolt tolerates no such abdication of responsibility. Every citizen of the kingdom of God is brought into the heat of the conflict between good and evil. Everyone who swears allegiance to Christ bears responsibility for humanity. The power and force of the barbarian way are that each one who chooses His path must find the courage to jump.

I wanted my son to have the courage to jump when needed. I am convinced God wants the same thing for us. Is it possible that your Father is also calling you to jump or at least encouraging you to do so? It is the Spirit of God stirring within you, pleading with you to stop settling for the status quo.

BEHIND ENEMY LINES

The way that we've applied the wrong metaphors in the wrong places is at least partially responsible for our inclination toward domesticating new believers. The Scriptures talk in terms of a new follower of Christ having undergone a new birth. The central passage for this image is John 3. Jesus was having a conversation with Nicodemus and said to him, "I tell you the truth. No one can see the kingdom of God unless he's born again."

Nicodemus immediately concluded that Jesus was calling him to reenter his mother's womb a second time. Instead of backing off, Jesus pressed harder: "I tell you the truth, no one can enter the kingdom of God unless he is born of water and the Spirit. Flesh gives birth to flesh, but the Spirit gives birth to spirit. You should not be surprised at my saying, 'You must be born again.' The wind blows wherever it pleases. You hear its sound, but you cannot tell where it comes from or where it is going. So it is with everyone born of the Spirit" (John 3:3–8).

This, of course, leads us to perceive people who are new in the faith as nothing more than brand-new babes. They're innocent and helpless and incapable of caring for themselves, much less serving others. Yet the phrase that Jesus used can also be translated not as "born again," but as "born from above." Jesus connected this birth not with a mother's womb, but with the Spirit of God descending from heaven and moving with power.

My point is this: the metaphor of new birth has led us to some wrong conclusions. When we are born of flesh and blood, we are helpless and dependent on others even for our own survival. That is not the case when we are born of Spirit. John spoke of the first birth as one of water and the second birth as one of Spirit. Strangely enough John the Baptist made a similar distinction in Luke 3:16 when he declared, "I baptize you with water. But one more powerful than I will come, the thongs of whose sandals I am not worthy to untie. He will baptize you with the Holy Spirit and with fire."

When we are born again, we are dropped not into a maternity ward, but into a war zone. Our birthplace is less mother's womb and more battlefield earth. Maybe the first word we hear should not be "welcome," but "jump." There is no trial run, no practice life.

KNIGHTS IN DARKNESS

When you enter the kingdom of God, there is no safe zone or waiting room. There really isn't even a boot camp. It's on-the-job, on-the-field training. You get to take your first steps of new life in the middle of the battlefield. The Scriptures are quite clear about this. You are in the middle of a war. Yet the war is not against flesh and blood; the war is not against people.

Paul said it this way: "Our struggle is not against flesh and blood, but against the rulers, against the authorities, against the powers of this dark world and against the spiritual forces of evil in the heavenly realms" (Ephesians 6:12).

The barbarian revolt is an insurrection that defies the treaty between civilization and the powers of the dark world. We will not stand by and watch humanity sell its soul to gain the world. We will not be seduced by the comforts offered us if only we would compromise. We cannot pretend that all there is, is what we can see. Barbarians know the world of spirit. We know there is a darkness that subversively corrupts the hearts of men, and to do nothing is to be complicit. We are born into a war. We may feel like children, but we are warriors.

Paul wanted to ensure that we know the nature of this conflict. He wrote, "For though we live in the world, we do not wage war as the world does. The weapons we fight with are not the weapons of the world. On the contrary, they have divine power to demolish strongholds. We demolish arguments and every pretension that sets itself up against the knowledge of God, and we take captive every thought to make it obedient to Christ" (2 Corinthians 10:3–5).

Paul reminded us that not only are we dropped into the middle of a war, but the war rages in the middle of us. You cannot run or hide from the war any more than you can run or hide from yourself. You can become a prisoner of war, but you are never exempt from the war.

It is true that the enemy will essentially leave you alone if you are domesticated. He will not waste his energy destroying a civilized religion. If anything, he uses his energy to promote such activity. Religion can be one of the surest places to keep us from God. When our faith becomes refined, it is no longer dangerous to the dark kingdom.

Barbarians, on the other hand, are not to be trusted. They respect no borders that are established by powers or principalities. They have but one King, one Lord, and one mission. They are insolent enough to crash the gates of hell. For the sake of others, they are willing to risk their own lives and thrust themselves into the midst of peril.

HALO EFFECT

Years ago I learned about an avant-garde military technique used by the Special Forces described as HALO. HALO stands for "high altitude low opening." While parachuting of any kind is a risky enterprise, to add the feature of enemy fire shooting at you, picking you off like a sitting duck as you glide slowly to the ground, would make it more so. The sound of the airplane would inform the enemy that you are coming, and your slow descent would leave you helpless to defend yourself.

HALO had an answer to both problems. The plane would fly minimally at 25,000 feet and sometimes up to 40,000 feet where it was undetectable even by radar. When it was time to jump, your first instruction was not to open your parachute. You would literally move into a free fall. In a matter of seconds your terminal velocity would be 120 miles an hour, though you might hit speeds of up to 200 miles per hour. You open the chute at the last possible minute, with only enough time to save your life. With canopy deployment at 1,800 to 2,200 feet, there's just enough time to break your fall so that you land safely behind enemy territory. If you live, you get to fight the enemy.

I think this somehow is a more accurate metaphor of what it means to enter the kingdom of God, not to mention a far more dramatic picture of what it could mean to be born from above. When we become citizens of God's kingdom, we are of both heaven and earth. We become like God's HALO effect—high altitude low opening.

Paul told us that "God raised us up with Christ and seated us with him in the heavenly realms in Christ Jesus" (Ephesians 2:6). Just a few verses later he reminded us that "we are God's workmanship, created in Christ Jesus to do good works, which God prepared in advance for us to do" (Ephesians 2:10).

It's as if at the moment of our conversion, we were lifted beyond time into eternity. Seated with Christ in the heavenly realms, we can't get much higher in altitude than that. But then created by God to do good, to fulfill His purpose in the world, to advance His cause, we are God's ground troops dropped from eternity back into history. In the same world where we were once at home, we are now strangers and aliens. Where once we were enemies of God, we are now behind enemy lines.

The procedure that God chooses is clearly a low opening. After a moment of euphoria, we come crashing back down to earth, opening our chutes just soon enough to break our fall and allow us to land on the ground, advancing on enemy territory.

PRIMAL ATTIRE

Last year the men of Mosaic invited me to join them at an event set in the mountains called Highlander. In groups of twenty, the guys were divided into Scottish clans. I was a member of the one Irish clan, O'Hare (which, by the way, won the Highlander championship). On Saturday night I talked about the barbarian way. I happened to mention my admiration for the Celts. I pointed out that when the Celts went to war, they painted their bodies and wore only their primal attire—in other words, they were in the buff. You can only imagine what the Roman soldiers who warred against them, dressed in the finest battle gear, must have thought when they ran across those Celts. Maybe this reason and this reason alone explains why the Romans could never conquer the Celts. They didn't really want to catch them.

The point, of course, was for the men at the retreat to

shed their doubts, to shed their fears, to shed their timidity—
not to shed their clothes. But in a study of missing the point,
the next morning at the closing event, which happened to be
a tug-of-war in the middle of a pool of mud, one of the men
we now simply call "Nature Boy" showed up naked. Since it
was a Christian camp, he was instructed to put on some
clothes, so he threw on a shirt. I think once again he missed
the point.

By the start of the tug-of-war, he was again unveiled in his
full glory. One of my friends, John, was the first man in line
on the opposing team. He is an attorney and a highly educated professional. You can only imagine what he was thinking: *Hold tight, pull hard, and keep your eyes up.*

Oh, and by the way, when Nature Boy's clan saw their
fellow tribesman choose the barbarian way, they stripped
in his honor. You can only imagine the whelps that resulted
from pulling rope against raw flesh. Fortunately what
their clan had in boldness, they lacked in muscle. Soon
they were covered in mud, their nakedness to be seen no
more.

When David returned to Jerusalem exhilarated by the
victories that God had given him at war, he disrobed and

danced before the Lord. But Michal, his wife, despised him. When she rebuked him for his inappropriate display of celebration and worship of God, David's answer was unwavering: "I will celebrate before the LORD. I will become even more undignified than this, and I will be humiliated in my own eyes" (2 Samuel 6:21–22).

I'm not saying that we should all go around naked, but I am saying that we need to find the courage and freedom to be ourselves. We need to let ourselves become the unique individuals that God created us to be. We need to stop trying to be what everyone else wants us to be and stop worrying about what everyone else thinks. Civilized people measure one another by their robes and signet rings. The barbarians measure only heart and actions. Barbarians live as if they are naked before God and naked before men. They have nothing to hide; they do not waste their energy pretending to be someone they're not. It was Nathaniel, whom Jesus saw while he was alone under a fig tree, that He described as a man without guile. God sees straight through to the heart and looks for those in whom there is nothing false. The barbarian hides nothing before God, and his tribe battles naked and unashamed.

WHEN TIGERS UNITE

Although the force of one person fully committed to God is tremendous, it pales in comparison to the force of God's people moving together. One barbarian wandering through civilization can be discarded as nothing more than an oddity. But when members of the barbarian tribe line up across the battlefield, side by side, something amazing begins to happen. Dark kingdoms tremble; the dungeons and prisons that hold men, women, and children captive crumble; prison doors open; chains unlock; and multitudes come to freedom. Whenever the barbarians of Christ pass through civilization, the oppressed and forgotten are soon found dancing in the streets.

When an opponent beheads one barbarian, he better be prepared, for we will return in force. We fight violence with peace, hatred with love, and oppression with servanthood. While never violating our uniqueness, we move together, united in heart and soul. Our greatness is unleashed in the context of community. When we move together, God is most perfectly revealed in us.

George Hunter in *The Celtic Way of Evangelism* describes

one reason why the Roman civilization was able to advance its empire, but the Celtic tribes were not. He uses an analogy given to him by a zoologist: "A tiger will defeat a lion in battle; but five lions will defeat five tigers because the lions fight together and the tigers do not, so the five lions take on one tiger at a time. Each Celtic tribe was a formidable tiger in battle, greatly respected and feared. The Romans, with legendary strength in organization and coordination, were the lions in the lengthy series of battles against specific tribes to incrementally expand their empire" (p. 18).

From the first moment I read that, I recognized the dilemma. Barbarians are far more tiger than lion. I am convinced the old adage is true, at least in this case, that a tiger can never change its stripes. More than that, we do not want to domesticate the tiger. We don't even want the tiger to try to become more like the lion. But imagine what it would be like if tigers could learn how to move together, if tigers would choose to stand side by side and engage in battle as one tribe.

Again the Scriptures describe the movement of the church as an unstoppable force. The expansion of God's invisible kingdom is the result of those of us who are passionate followers of Jesus Christ moving together united in heart, mind, and spirit. Jesus' description that "the kingdom of heaven has been forcefully advancing, and forceful men lay hold of it" (Matthew 11:12) is a call for tigers to move together, not for our untamed faith to be domesticated.

CRASH THE FUTURE

A few years ago I took my kids to a wildlife animal park near San Diego. As we rode on a tram through the open terrain, a guide pointed out the unique features of the different species that we encountered. I suppose I always knew it in part, but I had not come to realize how most groups of animals have unique names or designations when they dwell together.

With insects most of us know that bees are called swarms, and ants are called colonies. Among ocean life, I was aware that whales are pods, and fish are schools. Cattle are herds, birds are flocks, and if you watch *Lion King*, you know a tribe of lions is a pride. If you grew up in the country, you might know that crows are murders. Maybe the most unnerving one is an ambush of tigers.

I was surprised to learn that a group of buzzards waiting around together to feast on leftover carnage is called a committee. Just this one insight is worth the price of the whole book. This explains so much of what's going on in churches—a lot of committees waiting around to live off human carnage.

Groups of flamingos are called flamboyants, which for some reason reminds me of TV evangelists. And groups of the less glamorous owls are known as parliaments. They do seem sort of British.

But my favorite of all is the group designation for rhinos. You see, rhinos can run at thirty miles an hour, which is pretty fast when you consider how much weight they're pulling. They're actually faster than squirrels, which can run at up to twenty-six miles an hour. And even then, who's going to live in dread of a charging squirrel? (Sorry—that was a bit off the point.) Running at thirty miles an hour is faster than a used Pinto will go. Just one problem with this phenomenon. Rhinos can see only thirty feet in front of them. Can you imagine something that large moving in concert as a group, plowing ahead at thirty miles an hour with no idea what's at thirty-one feet? You would think that they would be far too timid to pick up full steam, that their inability to see far enough ahead would paralyze them to immobility. But with that horn pointing the way, rhinos run forward full steam ahead without apprehension, which leads us to their name.

Rhinos moving together at full speed are known as a crash. Even when they're just hanging around enjoying the watershed, they're called a crash because of their potential. You've got to love that. I think that's what we're supposed to be. That's what happens when we become barbarians and shake free of domestication and civility. The church becomes a crash. We become an unstoppable force. We don't have to pretend we know the future. Who cares that we can see only thirty feet ahead? Whatever's at thirty-one feet needs to care that we're coming and better get out of the way.

We need to move together as God's people, a barbarian tribe, and become the human version of the rhino crash. The future is uncertain, but we need to move toward it with confidence. There's a future to be created, a humanity to be liberated. We need to stop wasting our time and stop being afraid of what we cannot see and do not know. We need to move forward full force because of what we do know.

Yesterday Mariah was in a store with her mom. She saw a man working with fabrics, and for some reason he caught Mariah's attention. Mariah looked at Kim and pointed to the man, and she said, "Mom, look at the man. He's the loneliest person I've ever seen." Mariah began to weep uncontrollably.

We may not be able to see what's at thirty-one feet, but we don't have to be blind to what's right in front of us. There's a world that desperately needs God, a world filled with loneliness, hopelessness, and fear. We have somehow become deaf to a cry that reaches heaven coming from the souls of men. But God hears.

WARRIORS OF LIGHT

God heard the cries of Israel when the people lived under the tyranny of Egypt. And then He spoke and called out Moses. As one man, he went to war against an empire. He followed the barbarian way—a coward became a hero; a murderer became a deliverer; a shepherd became a prophet; a wanderer became a leader; an adopted son of Pharaoh became an adopted son of God; slaves became free—but before they became a nation, they had to learn how to survive the wilderness. The land of promise was not a land free from dangers. The milk and honey they were promised awaited them amid a land of giants.

It is no different for us. As it was for them, freedom is a return not to Paradise Lost, but to a promised land that we must win. Like Israel, who longed for Egypt because the journey was more difficult than the people expected, we must be aware of the temptation to return to the captivity from which we were freed. There is but one path to freedom. There is no easy road made available. We cannot claim to know Christ and to honor Him if we refuse the path He calls us to follow. Do not insist on binding Him or associating Him with a domesticated or civilized faith. Do not dishonor Him by claiming that a life of faith is a life without risk. This war has no room for pomp or pretension.

Jesus leads us into the heart of the dark kingdom, into the soul of what is most evil. He takes us where mankind has chosen to live. He calls us to where the darkness has made those who wander there desperate for light. He leads us as warriors of light to risk our lives for the deliverance of others. Again, our own weapons are love, hope, and faith, and they are our only defense. Yet we above all know that they and only they liberate us and fulfill the deepest longings of our souls.

If you choose to live your life in this way, if you make the insane decision to live your life for the sake of others, if you choose to follow the One whose barbarian path led Him to the brutality of the Cross, and if you embrace His invitation to take up your own cross and follow Him, then it has begun. If you dare allow God to unlock your primal spirit, He will unleash the raw and untamed faith within. Then you will know you have chosen the barbarian way out of civilization.

Jephthah the Gileadite was a mighty warrior. His father was Gilead; his mother was a prostitute. Gilead's wife also bore him sons, and when they were grown up, they drove Jephthah away. "You are not going to get any inheritance in our family," they said, "because you are the son of another woman." So Jephthah fled from his brothers and settled in the land of Tob, where *a group of adventurers gathered around him and followed him.* (Judges 11:1–3 italics added)

ACKNOWLEDGMENTS

To Kim, whom I met on the barbarian way; my children, Aaron and Mariah, who allowed me to share their lives with all who read these words; Holly, who joined my team on the condition that I would make it my prayer that God would bring her the man of her dreams; Erik, who is now Holly's husband—lives up to the dream; Tammy Borrero, who makes it possible for us to accomplish our overwhelming endeavors; my community at Mosaic and my team at Awaken who help me maximize my effectiveness and multiply the contribution we make together to serve humanity.

Also thanks to the Willow Creek Association for helping

me to get this message out. I'm always grateful for Sealy Yates and the team at Yates & Yates, who are not merely agents, but advocates. I cannot possibly thank enough Jonathan Merkh, Brian Hampton, Kyle Olund, and the entire team at Thomas Nelson Publishers. And of course to Rick, Greg, Enrique, and Robert, who have made it possible for me to accomplish more than I ever could have alone. To all who choose the barbarian way, especially to those like Steve Johnson, Paul Johnson, and Dave Olson, who find barbarians walking alone and invite them to walk with their tribe, I will always be grateful to you guys and so many others like you.

Stay off the paved road,

ERWIN

ABOUT
THE
AUTHOR

E RWIN RAPHAEL MCMANUS is a storyteller, an activist, and a creative.

As the creative force behind McManus Studios, Erwin inspires each person to live their most heroic life through the power of story, beauty, and design. Erwin serves as the principle visionary and primary communicator of Mosaic in Los Angeles.

He is the author of *An Unstoppable Force*, a Gold Medallion Award finalist; *Chasing Daylight; Uprising: A Revolution of the Soul; The Barbarian Way; Stand Against the Wind; Soul Cravings;* and *Wide Awake.*

Erwin is a native of El Salvador and is a graduate of the University of North Carolina and Southwestern Theological Seminary. He holds a Doctorate of Humane Letters from Southeastern University.

He and his wife, Kim, live in Los Angeles have two children, Aaron and Mariah, and a foster daughter, Paty.

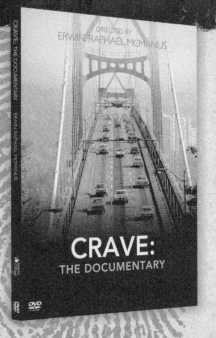

"I never realized our city was open to a spiritual conversation."

– Audience member, in Vancouver, BC, after watching Erwin McManus in *Crave: The Documentary*

YOUR CITY: Is it closed or open to the gospel? *Crave: The Documentary*, shot in Vancouver, BC, reveals the path to connecting to our deepest human longings. People are open to spirituality. In fact, they crave it. Filmmaker and philosopher Erwin McManus connects to the soul of the city and demonstrates in grippingly real conversations that people are open to Jesus.

△TEMPLE

by erwin raphael mcmanus

....

RECLAIMING A BRAVE PAST TO INSPIRE A HEROIC FUTURE

....

OUR RE-PURPOSED BAGS ARE RECONSTRUCTED
OUT OF AUTHENTIC RECLAIMED WWII DUFFELS. THEY ARE
HAND CRAFTED IN LOS ANGELES WITH CARE. YOU CAN COUNT
ON THEM TO LAST THROUGH ALL YOUR JOURNEYS.
ADVENTURE BEGINS WITH TEMPLE.

WWW.TEMPLEBAGS.COM